Cutting the Costs of Crime

The Economics of Crime and Criminal Justice

D. J. PYLE
Dean of Social Sciences
University of Leicester

Published by
INSTITUTE OF ECONOMIC AFFAIRS
1995

First published in November 1995

by

THE INSTITUTE OF ECONOMIC AFFAIRS
2 Lord North Street, Westminster,
London SW1P 3LB

© THE INSTITUTE OF ECONOMIC AFFAIRS 1995

Hobart Paper 129

All rights reserved

ISSN 0073-2818

ISBN 0-255 36373-7

Typography by Stuart Blade Enterprises

Cover design by David Lucas

Printed in Great Britain by
GORON PRO-PRINT CO LTD, LANCING, WEST SUSSEX
Set in Baskerville Roman 11 on 12 point

CONTENTS

FOREWORD

Crime statistics are always headline news. Debate rages about whether movements in 'recorded' and in actual crime are similar and analysts attempt to determine the reasons both for short-term changes and for more fundamental underlying trends.

Some economists, most notably Nobel Prize winners Professor Gary Becker and the late Professor George Stigler of the University of Chicago, have used economic theory to throw light on such issues as why people commit crimes, what is likely to deter them, and how penalties should be designed. Other economists have used econometric methods to test these theories.

In *Hobart Paper* No.129, Dr David Pyle, of the University of Leicester, who is one of Britain's leading researchers in the economics of crime, provides both a survey of recent research and some suggestions for action. He begins (Section II) with a review of international crime statistics and an analysis of crime figures in England and Wales (where the recent trend in recorded crime appears to be downward). He discusses also the costs of crime and outcomes of the criminal justice system (such as clear-up rates and changes in the prison population).

Section III of the *Paper* starts from the seminal work of Becker – crimes will be committed if expected benefits (adjusted for risk) exceed the expected benefits of 'legitimate' activity. Dr Pyle then discusses more recent theoretical work and econometric tests of theories about deterrence. He concludes that the evidence supports '...the view that crimes are deterred by increases in both the likelihood and severity of punishment'. There may also be a link between crime (particularly property crime) and general economic activity.

Dr Pyle turns, in Section IV, to economists' work on punishment – for instance, the design of penalties, how penalties for less serious offences should relate to those for the more serious, and how penalties for attempts at crime should relate to those for completed crimes. Using that work, he criticises the 'just deserts' principle of the Criminal Justice Act 1991 because it will '...not necessarily minimise the social cost

[5]

of crime and its control' (p.41). He points out also that, though research by economists generally supports emphasising fines (rather than imprisonment) and relating those fines to the offender's wealth, the 'unit fines' reform in the 1991 Act was soon rescinded.

Various forms of privatisation – in crime prevention, policing and prisons – are discussed in Sections V and VI, and American experience is outlined. As Dr Pyle points out, there does seem to be scope for market solutions. There is '...no reason in principle why privatisation of some parts of the criminal justice system should not lead to significant cost savings and increased efficiency' (pp.60-61).

Privatisation has had such effects in other markets and, he argues, '[t]here are few areas of crime control and policing where privatisation could not be tried' (p.61). In Dr Pyle's view, the problem is to overcome 'prejudice and vested interest' because solutions will come '...when the consumer can choose to buy protection in the market place'.

As always, the views expressed in this *Hobart Paper* are those of the author not of the IEA (which has no corporate view), its Trustees, Advisers or Directors. But both expert and lay observers will find great value in David Pyle's concise account of research findings and his discussion of market-based remedies.

October 1995   COLIN ROBINSON
Editorial Director, Institute of Economic Affairs;
Professor of Economics, University of Surrey

THE AUTHOR

DAVID PYLE is Dean of the Faculty of Social Sciences at the University of Leicester, where he is also a member of the Department of Economics. He is a former Economic Advisor and consultant to the Home Office.

His research interests in the last few years have been concentrated upon the economic analysis of law and especially the economics of crime and criminal justice. He has written widely on this subject, including two books: *The Economics of Crime and Law Enforcement* (Macmillan, 1983) and *Tax Evasion and the Black Economy* (Macmillan, 1989); and numerous articles in journals such as *Public Finance*, the *International Review of Law and Economics*, the *Scottish Journal of Political Economy* and the *British Journal of Criminology*.

Currently, he is writing a book about *Economic Reform in China*.

I. INTRODUCTION

Crime and the fear of crime have become major social issues. However, these phenomena are neither new nor confined to the UK, but are recurrent themes in the post-war experience of the advanced industrialised economies of Western Europe and North America. Fear of becoming the victim of crime has become so great in some places, that there are areas of many major cities into which ordinary people are now unwilling to venture, especially at night. Women, in particular, are urged to carry personal alarms in case they are attacked. It is now commonplace for city dwellers to spend their evenings barricaded behind bolted doors and windows, their homes also fitted with security lighting and burglar alarms. Car theft has become so widespread that anti-theft devices, such as car alarms and immobilisers are often fitted as standard on new cars.[1] As a result of measures such as these, once peaceful streets now reverberate to the sound of shrieking car and burglar alarms.

Maybe these are some of the more extreme manifestations of the consequences of increasing crime. Nevertheless, crime imposes considerable costs upon society, not only direct costs (the losses suffered by the increasing number of victims) but also indirect costs – those borne by individuals who attempt to avoid becoming victims of crime and by taxpayers who fund the activities of the criminal justice system (the police, courts, probation and prison services). This *Hobart Paper* contends that criminal justice policy should aim to reduce these cost consequences of crime in an economically efficient manner.

The paper analyses economic aspects of crime and criminal justice policy. It may seem surprising that economists have anything to say about the commission of crime or indeed about its control. But, over the last 25 years or so, economists have been researching the causes of crime and the design of penalties to deter criminals. This paper presents the conclusions of that research effort. In particular, it tries to

---

[1]   Indeed, one can even purchase 'fake' car and home alarms. - ED.

draw policy conclusions concerning the most effective ways in which to deal with crime.

Section II presents essential background information on crime and criminal justice policy, particularly in the United Kingdom. The UK is chosen to illustrate the nature of a problem which has afflicted many other advanced, industrialised economies in the last 20 years: information for these other countries is also presented.

Examination of the work of economists on crime begins in Section III, which considers the economic approach to crime, based on a view of criminals as rational individuals who respond to incentives. This section considers a number of issues, such as the extent to which criminals are deterred by increases in the certainty and severity of punishment (a special case of which is the deterrent effect of capital punishment) and the relationship, if any, between criminal activity and the state of the economy.

Section IV deals with the economic approach to punishment. Economists have attempted to determine an economically efficient structure of punishments for crimes. Issues discussed here include the relationship between 'efficient' and 'just' penalties, the concept of marginal deterrence, and how repeated offences should be punished.

In Section V privatisation in the criminal justice system, including privatisation of prisons and some policing functions, is discussed.

Conclusions about the design of criminal justice policy and the contribution which economics can make to this are in Section VI.

II. HISTORICAL AND STATISTICAL BACKGROUND

The main purpose of this section is to provide information on trends in crime, detection rates and resources used in law enforcement, particularly since the end of the Second World War, and to help set the scene for the subsequent discussions of crime and criminal justice policy. It also provides the context within which the theoretical and empirical contributions of economists writing in this area can be understood. The statistics relate mainly to Great Britain, whose experience is typical of many other advanced industrialised countries. But, before turning to Britain, crime statistics for a selection of developed economies are examined.

Increases in Crime World-wide

As Table 1 indicates, increasing crime rates are a world-wide phenomenon. Increases in *recorded* crime are common to the industrialised economies of Western Europe and North America.[1] Whilst there are some differences in the rates of increase shown in Table 1, all but those for the United States indicate rapid growth in recorded crime. Of course, *records* may not accurately measure true levels of crime. Not all crime is reported to, and recorded by, the police. For various reasons, some victims are unwilling to refer crimes to the police (Mayhew *et al.*, 1993). Some criminologists prefer, therefore, to construct indices of criminal acts from so-called victim surveys.

Instead of looking at recorded crime rates, Table 2 shows crime *victimisation* rates for the same seven countries as in Table 1, based on responses in a sample survey of households taken in each country.[2] Some of the crimes reported in a vict-

---

[1] Further information can be found in *Criminal Statistics, England and Wales, 1993*, Cm.2680, London: HMSO, Tables 1.2 and 1.3.

[2] The figures in Table 2 are taken from the latest International Crime Survey (ICS): see Van Dijk and Mayhew (1992). The ICS is based on responses to approximately 2,000 telephone inquiries in each of a number of countries. Interviewees are asked whether they have been the victim of a crime in the last

TABLE 1:
Increases in Recorded Crime in Selected
Industrialised Economies, 1987-92

Country	Percentage Increase
England and Wales	44
Netherlands	12
Belgium	32
Finland	24
USA	7
Canada	20
Australia	19

Source: Criminal Statistics, 1993, Cm. 2680, HMSO, 1993.

imisation survey may not be reported to the police. Table 2 also shows changes in victimisation rates between 1988 and 1991. Whilst these figures are not perfectly correlated with the figures reported in Table 1, they show a similar picture. For example, in the European countries victimisation rates appear to be rising as rapidly as recorded crime figures, but in North America and Australia recorded crime seems to be growing much more rapidly than victimisation rates. Indeed, in the USA (which stands out from the other countries listed in the Table), victimisation rates appear to be falling. If the survey results are to be believed, Table 2 shows that the chance of being the victim of a crime is considerable. In 1991, in many of the countries listed in Table 2, individuals faced a nearly 30 per cent probability of being a victim of crime.

British Crime Statistics

In Great Britain recorded crime has increased substantially since the end of the Second World War. In England and Wales between 1946 and 1992, so-called notifiable (more serious) offences[3] rose elevenfold from 472,500 to nearly 5·6 million,

---

year. The figures in columns 2 and 3 of Table 2 show the percentage of respondents who claim to have been a victim on at least one occasion in the calendar years 1988 and 1991.

[3] Notifiable offences include offences of violence against the person, sexual offences, burglary, robbery, theft and handling of stolen goods, and criminal damage.

TABLE 2:
Crime Victimisation Rates in Selected
Industrialised Economies, 1988-91

Country	1988	1991	% Change
England and Wales	19·4	30·2	+56
Netherlands	26·8	31·3	+17
Belgium	17·7	19·3	+9
Finland	15·9	20·7	+26
USA	28·8	25·1	−13
Canada	28·1	28·4	+1
Australia	27·8	28·6	+3

Columns 2 and 3 show the percentage of respondents who claimed to have been a victim of crime within the last 12 months. Column 4 shows the percentage change between the figures for 1988 and 1991.

Source: Van Dijk and Mayhew (1992).

an average rate of increase of over 5 per cent per annum. In Scotland crimes known to the police increased sevenfold over the same period from just under 77,000 to almost 590,000 – by over 4 per cent per year.

The number of recorded offences fell slightly in 1993 (in England and Wales by about 65,000) and more strongly in 1994 (by about 5 per cent in England and Wales). The decline continued in the first half of 1995, so that over the last two and a half years recorded crime has fallen by nearly 10 per cent in England and Wales – the largest fall in recorded crime in the post-war period. Is this likely to represent the beginning of a long-term trend and what are the causes of the recent fall?

There have been several other years in the past (for example, 1973, 1978, 1979, 1983 and 1988) when recorded crime has fallen, but the decline has been confined to one or at most two years. The post-war history of recorded crime in England and Wales is illustrated in Figure 1 (all offences) and Figure 2 (offences of burglary and theft, which account for about 75 per cent of all recorded crime). The long-term picture is one of a rapidly rising trend, superimposed on which are short-term fluctuations.[4] It has been claimed that

---

[4] These fluctuations may be in response to improving economic circumstances (see Section III, below, pp.26-28).

these fluctuations are closely related to changes in the economy. When the economy booms, and GDP grows rapidly, recorded crimes against property (burglaries and thefts) tend to decrease, but when the economy enters a slump, and GDP falls, recorded crimes against property tend to increase.[5] Other possible explanations for the recent fall in recorded crime include improvements in car security, special police targeting operations, improved surveillance devices and changes in recording practices by police forces. As yet, it is much too early to say which of these factors is predominantly responsible for the changes that have taken place, although work by Deadman and Pyle (1995) suggests that a time-series econometric model can largely explain short-term changes in recorded crime in England and Wales between 1992 and 1995: perhaps one-half of the fall in recorded crime is due to short-term improvements in the economy.

Criminologists argue that recorded crime statistics do not provide an accurate picture of crime: the real picture, they claim, may be either worse or better than painted by official statistics. The bad news is that only a proportion of crimes is reported to, and hence recorded by, the police. As a result, the real total of crimes is much larger than the official statistics suggest. However, the good news is that the number of recorded crimes may be growing more rapidly than the 'true' number of crimes, perhaps because the public is now more willing to report crimes to the police (though Tables 1 and 2 give a different view).

The extent of the bad news can be gleaned from the British Crime Survey (BCS), which samples approximately 10,000 households every few years. The latest Survey, carried out in 1992, suggests that true crime levels may be three times as high as the official statistics imply (Mayhew, Maung and Mirrlees-Black, 1993). In other words, there may be as many as 15 million crimes each year in England and Wales. However, some good news can be found in *Criminal Statistics 1993*, which suggests that between 1981 and 1993 the increase in 'true' crime (based on victim survey data) was 77 per cent compared with a 115 per cent increase in the number of crimes recorded by the police. The biggest discrepancy was in the growth of violent crime. For property crime (burglary and theft) the rates of increase in both recorded and 'real' crime figures

---

[5]   See Section III, below, pp.26-28.

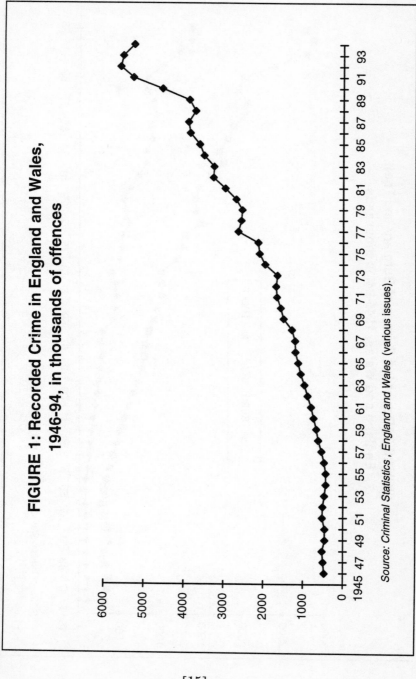

FIGURE 1: Recorded Crime in England and Wales, 1946-94, in thousands of offences

Source: Criminal Statistics, England and Wales (various issues).

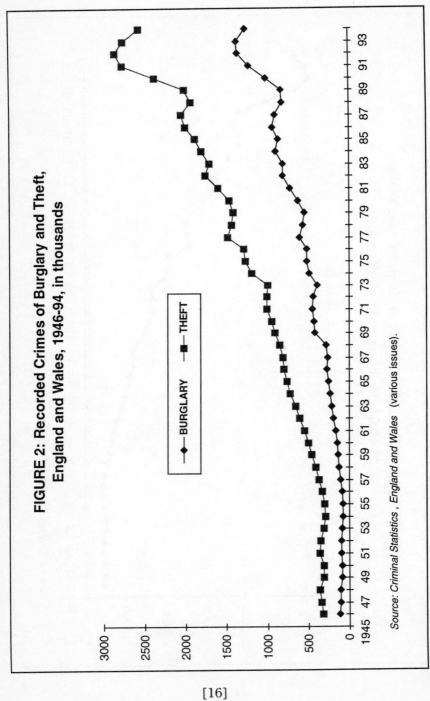

FIGURE 2: Recorded Crimes of Burglary and Theft, England and Wales, 1946-94, in thousands

Source: *Criminal Statistics*, *England and Wales* (various issues).

between 1981 and 1993 were similar (around 75 per cent). Most acquisitive property crime now appears to be reported to the police. For example, the 1992 BCS shows that virtually all thefts of motor vehicles and more than 90 per cent of burglaries involving losses were reported in 1991.[6]

Information on victimisation rates, whether from the International Crime Survey (ICS) or the BCS and information from recorded crime statistics all point strongly in the same direction.[7] The number of crimes occurring in Great Britain is growing rapidly so that, though under-reporting exists and part of the increase in recorded crime is probably due to an increase in the propensity to report offences, trends in recorded crime are not as misleading as some criminologists have suggested.

Costs of Crime in Britain

Crime imposes major economic costs. For example, there are the financial costs to victims, in terms of property lost or damaged.[8] In 1992 property worth approximately £1,000 million was reported stolen in the course of burglaries in England and Wales. Of this, only some £64 million has so far been recovered. In the same year, some £2·7 billion worth of property was stolen by thieves, about £1·8 billion in the form of stolen motor vehicles. The recovery rate for car theft is much higher than for burglary, so £1 billion worth of property

---

[6] Reporting rates are much lower for crimes such as vandalism, assault and household theft: only about one quarter of offences are reported to the police. The reasons for failing to report crimes are complex. However, common explanations, advanced by respondents to the BCS, include claims that the offence was too trivial and that the police would be unwilling to do anything.

[7] The International Crime Survey (ICS) figures suggest that 'true' crime rates are actually growing faster in England and Wales than the recorded crime statistics say they are (see Tables 1 and 2). However, the ICS is based on quite a small sample and therefore may be subject to some small sample bias.

[8] Some might argue that theft is really only a transfer 'payment' and so does not impose a real cost on society. However, this ignores the contested nature of the transfer. Some individuals invest resources in trying to defend their property, whilst other individuals invest their time and skills in trying to acquire the property of others. If individuals are rational and risk neutral, then both victim and criminal are prepared to invest £x in order either to defend or steal £x respectively. The total amount of resources invested in contesting the transfer is then £2x. This represents the extent of the cost to society.

was returned to the owners.[9] The value of stolen property fell slightly in 1993 to about £3·4 billion, of which £1·1 billion was recovered. Even if the prices criminals can obtain for selling stolen goods are only a fraction of their market price, the turnover of the crime industry is still enormous.

In addition to these costs are the considerable resources devoted to law enforcement. The cost of police, courts, probation and prison services was approximately £14·5 billion in 1993. This constitutes more than 5 per cent of total government expenditure and represents a substantial increase both in absolute terms and as a percentage of government spending, since 1982. The UK criminal justice system employed more than 250,000 people in 1992 – an increase of more than 50 per cent since 1971.[10]

Criminal Justice Outcomes

Despite the substantial increase in resources devoted to policing in the last 20 years or so, the proportion of recorded crimes solved (officially 'cleared up'[11]) has declined quite markedly. In 1976 more than 40 per cent of crimes were cleared up by the police; by 1992 this rate had dropped to barely more than a quarter.

Clear-up rates vary considerably across offences. High clear-up rates usually occur where the victim can identify the offender, as in a rape, or where the detection of the crime identifies the offender (as in fraud, drug-related crime, or handling stolen goods). Moreover, some crimes, such as murder and rape, receive more attention from the police so that clear-up rates tend to be higher. As a consequence, viol-

---

[9] This information has been obtained from *Criminal Statistics, 1993*. (See detailed reference in footnote 1.) There are also emotional costs of the victims.

[10] Information on expenditure in the criminal justice system has been obtained from *Social Trends, 25, 1995*, London: HMSO, Table 9.35. Information on employment in the criminal justice system comes from *Social Trends, 24, 1994*, Table 12.35.

[11] An offence can be cleared up by one of two routes. Either an individual is charged, summonsed or cautioned, or an offence is admitted and taken into consideration by a court. Sometimes the police believe that they have sufficient evidence to prove a case but do not prosecute, for example, when the crime has been committed by a child(ren) under the age of criminal responsibilty or where the alleged perpetrator is believed to be dead.

TABLE 3:
Clear-Up Rates: England and Wales, 1946-93

Category of Crime	1946	1956	1966	1976	1988	1993
Violence	88	90	84	79	71	76
Sexual Offences	78	81	78	77	71	74
Burglary	36	40	35	34	26	19
Robbery	42	49	37	33	20	22
Theft	37	42	36	41	31	23
Fraud and Forgery	92	90	84	81	67	51

The clear-up rate is the number of crimes deemed to have been cleared up, expressed as a percentage of the number of recorded crimes.

ent crimes tend to have high clear-up rates, as do sexual offences, fraud and forgery. Crimes against property, which constitute the majority of crimes, have low clear-up rates. For example, the probability of a burglary being cleared up is extremely low. If survey evidence (see above) on the extent of crime is reliable, then real clear-up rates may be much lower than those declared, perhaps as low as 10 per cent overall.

Table 3 shows that clear-up rates have fallen for all categories of crime. The changes in the UK criminal justice system following the Police and Criminal Evidence Act 1984, may help to explain the fall after 1986, but the downward trend was in existence long before this date.[12]

As recorded crime rates have risen, receptions into prison and the average prison population have increased rapidly. In 1946, the average daily prison population in England and Wales stood at 15,789, but the total had risen to 45,817 by 1992, increasing nearly every year. The prison population in Scotland displayed a similar trend, increasing from 1,976 in 1946 to 4,897 in 1992. In fact, imprisonment, the most severe and costly penalty, is rarely used. Fines are by far the most common form of punishment but are obviously not suitable for all offences or offenders (see the discussion in Section IV of the economic approach to punishment, below, pp.30 ff.). Given the high cost of keeping someone in prison

---

[12] The Police and Criminal Evidence Act made it more difficult for the police to obtain a conviction, because standards of proof were tightened significantly.

[19]

TABLE 4:
Imprisonment Rates in European Countries,
as at 1 September 1991

Country	Prisoners per 100,000 Population
Netherlands	44·4
Sweden	55·0
Italy	56·0
Norway	59·0
Ireland	60·4
Belgium	60·5
Finland	62·6
Denmark	63·0
Germany	78·8
Portugal	82·0
France	83·9
Switzerland	84·9
Austria	87·5
Luxembourg	90·3
England & Wales	91·3
Spain	91·8
Scotland	95·2

Source: Council of Europe, *Penological Information Bulletin*, December 1992.

(estimated at £23,000 a year), it is important that cheaper solutions are given full consideration and ways of cutting the cost of imprisonment are investigated. In any case, imprisonment rates in the UK are already high compared with other Western European countries (Table 4).

III. THE ECONOMIC APPROACH TO CRIMINAL BEHAVIOUR

Theory

The economic approach to criminal behaviour rests on the assumption that most potential criminals are normal individuals. They are not mentally ill or physically deformed, as 19th-century criminologists seemed to believe, but sane people who respond to incentives. In his seminal work, Becker (1968), the 1992 Nobel Laureate, argued that someone will commit a crime if the expected net benefit (utility) from committing the crime exceeds the expected benefit (utility) derived from legitimate activity. From the analytical point of view, an important aspect of criminal activity is that it is inherently risky because of the possibility of being caught.[1] Becker claimed that potential criminals will be deterred from committing crimes by increases in (i) the *probability* of being caught and punished, and (ii) the *amount* of punishment if caught, because each reduces the expected utility from engaging in criminal activity.

More elaborate theoretical work (Ehrlich, 1973), using a model of the allocation of time between criminal and legitimate activity, indicated that other *economic* factors, such as earnings in legitimate work (and hence, indirectly, income tax rates), returns to criminal activity and the probability of unemployment, could affect crime rates. He assumed criminals maximise expected utility, which is a weighted average of utilities in two states of the world (being caught and getting away with it), with the weights determined by the probabilities of being caught and going free, respectively.

In each state of the world, utility depends on both consumption and leisure. Consumption is determined by earnings from 'work' and working time can be allocated to

---

[1] Becker's formulation of the problem facing the individual ignores any moral qualms he or she might have about such activity. For an attempt to incorporate such scruples into an economic model of criminal behaviour, see Block and Heineke (1975).

[21]

criminal activity and/or legitimate employment. Ehrlich assumes that the wage-rates in both forms of work are known with certainty. This is, of course, a simplification, for the return to criminal activity cannot be forecast perfectly accurately. In this model, a rise in the legal wage, a fall in the return to criminal activity and increases in both the probability and severity of punishment will all deter an individual from involvement in criminal activity.

Early theoretical work on criminal behaviour was constructed in a static, single period framework, with the probability of detection assumed to be fixed. However, Sah (1991) has formulated a dynamic model of criminal participation, in which individuals live for a finite time and their perceptions of the probability of punishment are determined by the proportions of criminals they know who are detected. Individuals' behaviour is then aggregated over the whole population to produce a model of the aggregate crime rate. The following important conclusions emerge about the behaviour of the aggregate crime rate:

- Past crime breeds future crime, other things being equal. The current aggregate criminal participation rate is higher the higher was the criminal participation rate in the past because a higher crime rate, with a fixed police budget, reduces the detection rate. The crime participation rate therefore increases because individuals know of more criminals escaping detection. A similar effect is produced when fewer resources were spent on criminal detection in the past.

- It follows that two societies where the factors affecting criminal activity are identical at a particular time can have quite different steady-state crime participation rates as a result of past differences in crime or criminal justice policies.

- It follows also that the short-term impact of a policy change (for example, an increase in the detection rate) is smaller than its long-run effect because of a sequence of indirect effects. For example, an increase in the detection rate deters criminals, in part, because they know of more people being caught. With a fixed policing budget now being used to investigate fewer crimes, the detection rate is further increased, which lowers the crime rate still more. In other words, a virtuous circle is established. Of course, a falling detection rate would trigger a vicious circle of rising crime.[2]

Evidence on Deterrent Effects

From the standpoint of criminal justice policy, it is important to estimate the quantitative effects which different variables, especially criminal justice variables, have on the crime rate. Accordingly, research in the economics of crime has switched from theoretical analysis of criminal behaviour to the estimation of so-called crime 'supply' equations.

In general the econometric evidence, admittedly mainly using recorded crime statistics, supports the view that crimes are deterred by increases in both the likelihood and severity of punishment (for a survey see either Cameron, 1988, or Lewis, 1986).[3] Most of this work has used data for the USA. British studies (Carr-Hill and Stern, 1979; Pyle, 1989; Willis, 1983; Wolpin, 1978a) have all used slightly different sets of statistics and rather different model specifications, but they all support the predictions of the theoretical models, especially concerning deterrent effects. They also indicate that the deterrent effect of certainty of punishment is stronger than the deterrent effect of its severity. Where the crime index has been disaggregated, it seems that punishment exerts a stonger deterrent effect for property crimes than it does for violent or sexual offences (Willis, 1983). Furthermore, within the general group of crimes against property (burglary, theft and robbery), deterrent effects differ quite substantially from one crime group to another (Pyle, 1989).

The finding that increases in detection rates exert a significant deterrent effect on the number of recorded crimes, raises the question of how the detection rate can be increased. In particular, what is the effect of an increase in police manpower or expenditure on the detection rate? The

---

[2] In order to generate these conclusions Sah assumes that stable, interior steady states are possible in his model.

[3] There have been several attempts to estimate economic models using data on individuals. For example, Witte (1980) estimated a model using data on convicts released from the North Carolina prison system. She found evidence of deterrent effects as well as positive influences of wages in legitimate employment.

evidence linking increases in police manpower and/or expenditure to increases in either detection or conviction rates is not strong.[4] Both Wolpin and Pyle report only a small, positive correlation between police resources and detection rates. For example, Wolpin found that a 1 per cent increase in the number of police *per capita* increased the conviction rate by 0·6 per cent. Pyle found that a 1 per cent increase in police manpower increased clear-up (detection) rates by between 0·15 per cent and 0.25 per cent and conviction rates by between 0·5 and 0·6 per cent, depending on the type of offence.

Pyle estimates the cost of reducing property crimes by 1 per cent by either (i) increasing police manpower, or (ii) sending more offenders to prison, or (iii) increasing the average length of imprisonment. The estimates suggest that both imprisonment options are considerably cheaper than increasing police numbers, despite the bigger response of criminals to certainty rather than severity of punishment.[5] One explanation for this apparent inconsistency may be that offences such as theft and burglary are not directly deterred by extra police patrolling. More police manpower can only deter these offences through an increase in the detection rate, which is difficult to achieve.

The Deterrent Effect of Capital Punishment

A special case of deterrence is the effect the death penalty might exert on the incidence of homicide – a topic of increasing importance as more and more states in the USA are voting to restore the death penalty. Economists have undertaken a detailed examination of this issue, following several papers by Ehrlich (1975, 1977).

---

[4] In fact, Carr-Hill and Stern found that increases in police manpower tended to *reduce* rather than increase the clear-up rate for *recorded* crime. They explain this rather odd result by arguing that increasing the number of police officers leads to more crimes being *reported* which are then difficult to solve. They refer to this as the 'creating' effect of increased policing. Of course, their finding is entirely consistent with there being an increase in the *number* of crimes solved.

[5] Pyle focuses on the public sector financial costs of the alternative options. As a result, he ignores the opportunity costs of prisoners' time. However, given the substantial cost differences (both imprisonment options cost in the region of £4 million, whereas the policing option is costed at £51 million), it seems unlikely that the inclusion of such costs would drastically alter his conclusions.

To determine whether or not capital punishment exerted a deterrent effect, Ehrlich used econometric methods to estimate so-called murder 'supply' equations. These equations included as explanatory variables a number of sanctions, socio-economic and demographic variables. Ehrlich claimed in his earlier paper, on the basis of time-series results for the USA between 1933 and 1969, that one more execution would deter approximately seven or eight murders.[6] In his later paper, using cross-section data for abolitionist and retentionist states in the USA, he claimed that the deterrent effect of execution might be even stronger: as many as 20-24 homicides might be deterred by a single execution. Wolpin (1978b) undertook a similar time-series, econometric study for the UK, using data between 1929 and 1968, and confirmed that capital punishment did exert a significant deterrent effect, with one more execution leading to perhaps four fewer homicides. Ehrlich's work has been severely criticised on the grounds that it failed to produce robust estimates of the deterrent effect of execution (Passell and Taylor, 1977; Klein, Forst and Filatov, 1978).[7]

Leamer (1983) and McManus (1985) have argued that researchers' prior beliefs about which social and economic variables are thought to influence the homicide rate could influence whether one finds evidence of a statistically significant effect of execution. For example, McManus argues that 'a rational maximiser' would claim that deterrence variables are important, but that social and economic factors are 'doubtful' explanatory factors. Likewise, someone believing that murder is a 'crime of passion' would claim that deterrence variables are doubtful, but that social and economic variables are important explanatory factors.

Using cross-section data for US states in 1950, McManus estimated murder supply equations for different prior beliefs.[8]

---

[6] The 90 per cent confidence interval was between 0 and 24 murders prevented per execution.

[7] For example, investigators discovered that Ehrlich's findings were quite sensitive to the functional form of the 'supply' equation (whether the equation was estimated in logarithms or natural values of variables) and to choice of the end-point (whether the sample period was either 1933-69 or 1933-66) of the data set.

[8] Five prior beliefs were investigated: 'right winger', 'rational maximiser', 'eye for an eye', 'bleeding heart' and 'crime of passion'. Each categorises the three sets of explanatory variables as either doubtful or important.

The economic variables were median family income, percentage of families with an income of less than one-half of median income, the unemployment rate, and the labour force participation rate. The social variables were the percentages of the population that were (i) non-white, (ii) aged 15-24 years, (iii) lived in urban areas, and (iv) male, and (v) the proportion of families with both husband and wife present. The sign, size and significance of the deterrence variables (conviction, imprisonment and execution) were found to vary according to the choice of the explanatory variable set.

Some economists have searched for alternative statistical methods of isolating a deterrent effect. Cover and Thistle (1988) and Deadman and Pyle (1989, 1993), working independently, turned to the method of 'intervention analysis' (previously used to examine the effects of legal reforms, such as the introduction of seat-belt legislation and gun control laws).[9] If most of the socio-economic and demographic factors and even the law enforcement variables affecting the homicide series change only slowly over time, then the homicide series itself will exhibit a considerable degree of inertia. Such a series could be modelled quite successfully by what statisticians call an Autoregressive Moving Average (ARMA) process. This is a model made up of a combination of lagged values of the dependent variable and error terms only (Granger and Newbold, Ch.1, pp.28-31). The advantage of time-series techniques over the standard econometric approaches, used by Ehrlich and others, is that they do not require a detailed model specification, including all of the variables thought to affect the dependent variable (the homicide rate). The 'intervention' – in this case the abolition of capital punishment – is then simply modelled as a structural break in

---

[9] Intervention analysis is a variant of time-series econometric modelling, in which the current value of a variable is modelled as a function of its own past values and a series of random errors. At the point of the intervention (in this case the abolition of capital punishment), the process modelling the variable (in this case the homicide rate) may be disturbed in some way. For example, there might be a permanent step change in the dependent variable. Alternatively, there may be only a temporary change or the movement to a new higher (lower) level may take place only gradually. Various kinds of intervention effects can be allowed and tested for. For a survey of this literature and an introduction to intervention analysis, see Pyle and Deadman (1993).

the time-series and standard statistical tests can be used to test whether the structural break is statistically significant.

Cover and Thistle (1988) examined time-series data for the USA between 1934 and 1984 and Canada between 1926 and 1986. They found no evidence of an intervention effect in either the USA or Canada. However, they admit that the result for Canada may be sensitive to the particular model specification chosen and that the period of abolition in the USA (1968-76) may have been too short for the series to have established a new 'equilibrium'. This latter problem can be overcome by choosing a country in which capital punishment has been abolished for a longer period, for example, the UK, where the death penalty was abolished in 1965.

Deadman and Pyle (1993) analysed data on the number of offences of homicide initially recorded by the police each year in England and Wales between 1880 and 1989 and in Scotland over the period 1884 to 1987. Their results are consistent with the hypothesis that there was a small, but nevertheless significant, increase in the number of homicides following the abolition of capital punishment – perhaps 30 additional homicides each year in England and Wales, and also in Scotland.

Crime and the Economy

The idea that crime may be related to economic factors like unemployment has proved particularly controversial. Economic models of criminal behaviour clearly suggest that factors such as unemployment and low income might *motivate* some individuals to engage in crime. On the other hand, in times of relative economic decline there are fewer *opportunities* for potential criminals. For example, stealing from employers may fall during a recession, if only because the number of people in employment has diminished.

Several extensive literature reviews of the relationship between crime and unemployment (Freeman, 1980; Tarling, 1982; Long and Witte, 1983; Box, 1987) have all reached similar conclusions – that the relationship is at best inconsistent. Chiricos (1987, p.188) has referred to this as 'the consensus of doubt', whilst Cantor and Land (1985) argue that it can be explained by the countervailing effects of criminal motivation and criminal opportunity (see above). However, it is difficult to believe that the opportunities effect is dominant in the face of increases in unemployment, at least in the short run. A drop in output will have only a small impact on the existing stock of 'stealable' items. Indeed, it would have no impact whatsoever on the most desirable crime targets (for example, antiques). The inconsistent effect of unemployment is more likely to represent the failure of modelling and estimation methods, rather than being evidence of the existence of countervailing effects.

Most econometric studies of the relationship between crime and unemployment in Britain find that unemployment has a significant, positive (although small) effect on recorded crime (Wolpin, 1978a; Willis, 1983; Pyle, 1989; Hale and Sabbagh, 1991; Reilly and Witt, 1992). A notable exception to this rule is the study by Carr-Hill and Stern (1979), although Hakim (1982) claims they '...reject the hypothesis about unemployment contributing to crime on theoretical...grounds' (p.452). Reilly and Witt claim there is an extremely robust link between crime and unemployment in Scotland but this claim is questioned by Pyle and Deadman (1994a). None of these studies tests whether there is a link between crime rates and either youth unemployment or hard-core (long-term) unemployment. In general, they focus on the overall unemployment rate.

Attention has turned away from the relationship between crime and unemployment to consider instead the rôle of other economic indicators, particularly consumers' expenditure (Field, 1990) and gross domestic product (Pyle and Deadman, 1994b). Recorded unemployment may no longer be a good economic indicator of the state of the business cycle in the UK, especially following the substantial revisions and redefinitions which occurred in the 1980s and subsequently. Moreover, unemployment lags behind the cycle in economic activity by, on average, between six and 12 months but sometimes by as much as two years. As a consequence, when the economy turns into a recession, manifesting itself in terms of reduced overtime, part-time working, reduced job *quality* and falling income, unemployment will not necessarily be rising. However, if property crime is a response to worsening economic circumstances, then it will already have begun to increase as reduced income and short-time working begin to reduce living standards (Allan and Steffensmeier, 1989). Thus, if property crime has economic determinants, other economic indicators, more closely related to the economic cycle than unemployment, will be more strongly correlated with recorded crime rates.

Field found evidence of an inverse relationship between the growth in real personal consumption and the growth in property crime, which was of only a short-term nature. In the long run, the rate of growth of crime showed no relationship to the rate of growth of real consumption. In the short run, a motivational effect seems to dominate, whilst in the long run, growth in consumption also increases the opportunities for crime, counteracting the motivational effect.

Pyle and Deadman (1994b) re-examined Field's data using modern time-series techniques. They focussed on property crimes (theft and handling of stolen goods, burglary and robbery) and also found evidence of a strong short-run relationship between the economy and recorded crime. However, they found that real GDP was much more strongly correlated with crime than was real personal consumption.

The studies of Field (1990) and Pyle and Deadman (1994b) suggest recorded crime, particularly recorded property crime, is much more closely correlated with the level of economic activity in England and Wales, at least in the short term, than had previously been thought. These studies, incorporating developments in the econometric analysis of time-series data, have re-affirmed a much earlier conclusion – that property crime is, in the short run, closely related to economic activity (Thomas, 1927, Henry and Short, 1954).

IV. THE ECONOMIC APPROACH TO PUNISHMENT

The economic analysis of punishment of convicted offenders, which is clearly related to and informed by the literature on the economic analysis of criminal activity, can also be traced to the work of Becker (1968). There has been less work undertaken in this area than in the analysis of crime but several issues have been addressed in a predominantly theoretical framework. Much has concerned the design of penalties for a single criminal act. Should a penalty be related to the harm caused by the offence (a 'just' sentence) or should it be determined by 'efficiency' criteria, that is, by its ability to deter an offender and so reduce the cost of crime?[1]

Designing Penalties

Punishment can serve several aims and it is hardly surprising that experts disagree over the importance of each. Economists working in the area of crime and punishment place considerable weight on the rôle of punishment as a deterrent to further criminal activity, although they are not advocating so-called 'deterrent' sentences, but rather economically efficient ones (see below, pp.34-35). However, the criminological literature on sentencing suggests other goals of punishment, such as rehabilitation, incapacitation, desert (or 'justice') and reparation (Ashworth, 1992). Of course, these aims are not necessarily in conflict. For example, a 'just' sentence may also deter, although not necessarily for as long as a deterrent sentence.

Economic theory suggests that, in certain extreme circumstances, the punishment for a less serious crime should exceed that for a more serious crime. However, this ignores an important issue: crimes may not be independent of one another, so that criminals may switch between crimes in response to differences in punishment. If more serious

---

[1] Becker thought that so-called 'efficient' and 'just' sentences were the same thing.

offences are not more severely punished, is there a danger that the criminal will receive distorted signals? For example, if the penalties for both rape and murder are life imprisonment, will rapists be tempted to murder their victims in order to reduce the chance that they are caught? Thus the structure of penalties for related offences requires consideration. This introduces the concept of marginal deterrence (Stigler, 1970).

An issue, related to the question of marginal deterrence, concerns the penalty for attempted crime and how this should be related to the penalty for the 'completed version' of the crime. For example, should one offer an incentive to the criminal to withdraw from a criminal activity already begun. If the penalty for an attempt is just as severe as that for the completed crime, then does such incentive exist?

The final question concerns the structure of penalties for repeated offences. In many countries, it is common practice to increase the penalty for a subsequent offence above that given to a first-time offender. Can such a policy be justified on either efficiency criteria or in the interests of justice?

Types of Punishment

Types of punishment are also important. Forms of punishment range from fines through probation, community service orders and eventually imprisonment, all with different resource cost. Fines, as essentially a transfer payment, are relatively costless, whilst imprisonment is relatively costly (the costs of incarceration plus the lost output of the prisoner). Punishments may also have different deterrent effects. Economists are interested in finding the optimum mix of punishments which minimises the cost of crime and its punishment: they tend to favour the more widespread use of fines, partly because they are cheaper than other forms of punishment, and some have recommended that fines be related to the wealth of the offender (Polinsky and Shavell, 1984).

The arguments developed by economists are as follows. If criminals are risk-neutral, then they will engage in crime only if the expected gain is larger than the expected penalty. Becker (1968) argued that fines impose no social cost, so that to minimise the combined cost of crime, criminal detection and punishment, one should increase the size of the fine and at the same time reduce the amount devoted to criminal detection, so that the probability of punishment falls whilst keeping the expected penalty constant. The logical conclusion is that the fine should be set equal to the offender's wealth (Polinsky and Shavell, 1984; Shavell, 1992),[2] though in practice there may be objections to such a policy (see the arguments below, pp.36-37, concerning marginal deterrence).

However, for some crimes – for example, murder or rape – a fine is impractical for several reasons. *First*, the fine would probably exceed the wealth of the offender. *Second*, it is debatable to what extent such violent acts could be deterred by a financial penalty. *Third*, for crimes of this type incapacitation of the offender is probably just as important as deterring other offenders and that can only be achieved by some form of custodial sentence (Shavell, 1985).[3]

A theory of 'optimum sentencing' developed by Waldfogel is explained in Box 1 (below, pp.34-35). The conclusion of this work is that 'efficient' prison sentences (those which minimise the costs of crime and its control) are not necessarily 'just', in the sense that they may be only indirectly related to the harm caused by the crime concerned. An economically efficient sentence also takes into account the deterrent effect of the sentence.

Waldfogel has used the results of empirical studies to estimate optimum prison sentences for larceny, robbery and auto-theft in the USA, on the assumption that E_i (the elasticity of a crime with respect to the length of imprisonment for that crime) is constant for each crime, although it may vary across crimes. Estimates of E_i are drawn from three studies of crime deterrence in the USA (reported in a survey by Lewis, 1986), whilst estimates of harms (D_i) are taken from a study by Cohen (1988). Estimates of b (the unit cost of imprisonment) and p_i (the probability of imprisonment) are based on information published by the Department of Corrections in the USA. The estimated optimum prison sentences are found to be rather longer than actual average sentences. For example, for the crime of robbery, the actual sentence is 31 months, but the optimum sentence is estimated to be approximately six years.[4]

---

[2] As a result the rich would pay larger fines than the poor.

[3] A combination of a fine and a period of imprisonment might be a possible alternative.

[4] Waldfogel made an arithmetical mistake in calculating the optimal sentences. He erroneously believed that the estimated optimum sentences were in units of

TABLE 5:
Normalised Harms and Time Served

Crime	Implicit Harm	Cohen's Harm	Time Served
Murder	910·1	629·6	7·7
Rape	52·2	16·3	4·1
Assault	0·5	3·8	1·8
Robbery	15·1	4·0	2·9
Burglary	0·1	0·4	1·5
Larceny	0·3	0·1	1·0

Source: Waldfogel (1993). Harms and time served are expressed relative to those of auto-theft. As a result auto-theft would appear as 1·0 in each column and has therefore been excluded.

Waldfogel's choice of measure to proxy D, the damage caused by crime, might be questioned. Cohen's estimates are based on the money values of property stolen. As a consequence, the 'efficient' sentence for car theft exceeds that for robbery, but many people would feel that robbery is a rather more serious crime than auto-theft. Of course, this does not invalidate Waldfogel's theoretical analysis, but merely argues for a different and perhaps rather more appropriate measure of damage (D).

Whilst actual prison sentences in the USA are somewhat shorter than the optimal sentences calculated by Waldfogel, he is careful to play down attempts to test the efficiency of the criminal justice system in this way on the grounds that the assumptions needed to calculate optimal sentences are quite severe. Instead, he concentrates on estimating the harms *implicit* in the actual sentences imposed by the courts. This can be done by using equation (2) to find D_i, given x_i, b, p_i and E_i. When normalised (on the estimate of the harm caused by auto-theft), these are claimed to be quite close to normalised versions of Cohen's estimates of the harms caused by crime (see Table 5). Waldfogel argues that 'proportional justice' requires that normalised harms should be equated with norm-

[*continued on p.36*]

---

months. They are in fact in units of years. Therefore, the figures quoted here are twelve times larger than those found in Waldfogel's paper. The optimum sentences for larceny and auto-theft are estimated at about 17 months and seven years respectively.

BOX 1

The Theory of Optimum Sentencing

To illustrate the theory of optimum sentencing we use a model due to Waldfogel (1993) who argues that an 'efficient' set of punishments (which he assumes are prison sentences)[1] should aim to minimise the social cost of crime and its control. It is assumed that only one form of punishment is possible.

The cost function is of the form:

$$C = D [C_1(x_1), C_2(x_2),......, C_n(x_n)] + b \Sigma p_i C_i x_i \quad (1)[2]$$

where

$D [ ]$ is the social damage function, which relates the harm caused by crime to both the number and type of crimes committed;[3]

C_i is the number of crimes of type i. For example, C_1 could be the number of burglaries, C_2 the number of murders and so on;

x_i is the length of imprisonment for a crime of type i;

p_i is the probability of imprisonment for crimes of type i; and

b is the unit cost of imprisonment.

Explicit in equation (1) is the assumption that the number of crimes of type i (C_i) depends on the length of imprisonment for that crime (x_i) only and not on punishments for other types of crime (x_i). In other words, there are no cross-substitution effects of punishment. This assumption is relaxed when considering marginal deterrence.

The social cost of crime consists of two elements. *First*, the harm caused by crime itself, which is given by the function $D [ ]$, and *second*, the resource cost associated with punishment, which is given by the second term in (1) $b\Sigma p_i C_i x_i$.[4] For simplicity the cost of apprehending offenders is excluded. Expression (1) can be minimised by choice of x_i. This leads to a set of optimum lengths of imprisonment ($x_i{}^*$), given by

$$x_i{}^* = - D_i.E_i / bp_i (1 + E_i) \quad i = 1,.....,n \quad (2)$$

where

D_i is the marginal social harm caused by an additional crime of type i, and E_i is the elasticity of crimes of type i with respect to the length of imprisonment for that crime. That is, $E_i = (\delta C_i/\delta x_i)(x_i/C_i)$, which shows the percentage response of crime to a one percentage point change in the length of imprisonment.

Normally an increase in sentence length would be expected to deter offences and so $E_i < 0$ (see Section II, above, pp.23-24). Given that it is only meaningful for $x_i{}^*$ to be positive, then equation (2) requires that $E_i > -1$.

As can be seen from equation (2), unless E_i, b and p_i are all constant, then $x_i{}^*$ will not be directly related to D_i, the harm caused by the offence. More importantly, if E_i and p_i vary across crimes, then relative sentence lengths (x_i^*) will not necessarily be related to relative harms (D_i). For example, if more serious offences are less easily deterred by punishment and are also more likely to be punished, then prison sentences will increase less than proportionately with the harm caused (low values of E_i and high values of p_i in equation (2) would offset the effect of a larger D_i upon x_i^*). Indeed, it is possible that a more serious offence could, under perhaps extreme assumptions, receive a less severe penalty.

Consider the following numerical example. The marginal damage associated with crime i (say, a theft) is £100. The values of E_i, p_i and b are -0·5, 0·5 and £200 per year respectively. Using equation (2) we find that the optimum value of x_i is one year. For crime k (say, a burglary), D_k is £200 and E_k and p_k are -0·1 and 0·5 respectively, whilst the cost of imprisonment (b) remains £200 per year. The optimum length of imprisonment for crime k is then approximately three months. In other words, economic efficiency requires that the more serious offence, in terms of the damage caused, is punished by a lighter prison sentence. The explanation for this rather odd result is that the more serious offence is much less easily deterred by punishment. Of course, if the elasticities of response of crime to punishment are the same for each crime, then the more serious offence will be punished by a longer prison sentence, other things being equal. More important in explaining this counter-intuitive result is the assumption that criminals are not induced to switch between criminal acts by differences in sentence lengths. That is, thieves do not turn to burglary in response to more lenient sentences for burglars.

---

1 The punishment in Waldfogel's model need not be imprisonment. Any other form of punishment could be substituted for imprisonment, provided it involves some real resource cost.

2 This formulation is very similar to Becker's (1968), except that Becker includes the cost of apprehending offenders and does not specify the form of the punishment involved. Neither of these changes makes any material difference to the answer. The model could be generalised to allow for different forms of punishment (by allowing b to vary according to the form of the punishment). In the extreme case, to which Becker pays most attention, the punishment is by fine, in which case b = 0.

3 The function D[ ] may be non - linear to allow for either diminishing or increasing marginal harm caused by crime.

4 If C_i is the number of crimes of type i committed, then p_iC_i is the number of criminals who are caught and punished for type i crimes. Finally, $p_iC_ix_i$ is then the number of person years these individuals spend in prison; when multiplied by b and summed over the n types of crimes this gives the total cost of keeping offenders in prison.

alised sentences.[5] However, the implicit normalised harms are claimed to be quite different from those based on this notion of proportional justice (see Table 5). He argues, therefore, that in the USA actual sentences are more closely related to efficient sentences than they are to just sentences. This conclusion might be rather different if the crime of murder was removed from the list in Table 5. It would then appear that the relativities established in column 3 (by time served) are rather closer to those of column 2 (Cohen's estimates of relative harm) than those given in column 1.

One might have reservations about using Cohen's estimates of the cost of crime to measure the harms inflicted by crime and therefore their use as a benchmark for judging whether sentences were 'efficient' or 'just'. Despite these reservations, Waldfogel's paper has helped to sharpen the debate over 'justice' versus 'efficiency'. If nothing else it makes one consider rather more explicitly the goals of punishment and the costs of pursuing those particular objectives.

Marginal Deterrence

In the last section we found that economic analysis generated the slightly implausible result that in certain, perhaps rare, circumstances a more serious crime might be punished by a less severe prison sentence. In part, this result is explained by the assumption that crimes are independent of one another – that is, the number of crimes of a certain type is dependent only on the punishment for that crime and not on the punishments for other types of crime. In this section that assumption is relaxed, although for simplicity the analysis is restricted to only two types of crime.

One problem with the result obtained in the previous section is the risk that a criminal might switch from a crime with a high punishment to one with a low punishment. If the 'worse' (more harmful) crime is punished by a shorter prison sentence, the criminal justice system might produce strange incentives, inducing individuals to switch from less serious to more serious crimes. It may be necessary to structure punishments so that such an incentive cannot exist. In other

---

[5] 'Just' sentences require that $x_i = a\, D_i$, where a is a factor of proportionality that converts harm into sentence length. If sentences were set in this way, it would follow that $D_i/D_j = x_i/x_j$, provided that a does not vary across crimes.

words, an element of *marginal* deterrence (Stigler, 1970) should be retained. It may also be necessary to do this where a criminal might be induced to commit a more serious crime in order to escape detection for the less serious one (the robber who kills his victim).

Since Stigler there has been a strong presumption in the literature on the economics of punishment that the criminal justice system should '... keep the punishment for the less serious crime down so as not to tempt offenders to switch to the more serious [crime]' (Friedman and Sjostrom, 1993, p.365). But more formal economic analysis of marginal deterrence (Friedman and Sjostrom, 1993; Shavell, 1992) fails to provide complete support for the idea that more serious offences should be punished more severely, unless special assumptions are made.

This might not be as damaging to the concept of marginal deterrence as might appear. For example, in discussing situations in which the criminal is choosing among alternative crimes, Friedman and Sjostrom show that the optimum penalty for the more serious crime will always exceed that for the less serious crime if the more serious crime also yields larger benefits to the criminal and the number of offenders is finite. The first of these assumptions seems relatively harmless and would generally be the case for many property crimes. In the situation where the criminal's objective in committing the more serious crime is to make it harder for him or her to be caught, Shavell (1992) has argued that marginal deterrence could be achieved by setting cumulative sanctions for the commission of multiple harmful acts. For example, he argues that as long as

'...there is a sanction for murder that is added to the sanction for kidnapping, there will be a reason for the kidnapper not to commit the additional crime of murder; [and] this will be true whether or not the sanction for murder alone is higher than that for kidnapping alone' (p.351).

Punishing Attempts to Commit Crime

There are two main issues in the literature about attempts to commit crimes. *First*, should such attempts be punished at all? *Second*, if punishing attempts is justified, should the punishment be less than the punishment for the 'completed version' of the crime? Some of the arguments are reminiscent of the debate about marginal deterrence: the concern is to provide criminals with incentives not to undertake criminal acts and to abandon attempts.

The argument for punishing attempts is that it increases deterrence, particularly in situations where there is an upper limit on the penalty for a completed crime. As explained above, sentencing needs to preserve an element of marginal deterrence. Moreover, it may be cheaper to apprehend the perpetrators of attempts than it is to catch those who commit the completed crime.

Shavell (1985, 1990) argues that the penalty for an attempted crime need not be less than the penalty for the completed crime itself. The penalty for attempted crime should only be less if the court possesses imperfect information concerning the specific acts. If the courts were perfectly informed, so they could calculate the expected harm associated with the attempted crime and the crime itself, then they would merely have to determine the penalties for (i) the attempt and (ii) the crime itself so as to make the expected punishment at least as large as the expected harm caused by the crime and the attempt to commit it. However, this approach is quite consistent with a penalty for the attempted crime greater than, equal to or less than the penalty for the crime itself. In some cases (where, for example, expected harm is low) it may be sufficient to punish the completed crime only.[6]

When the courts possess imperfect information (as, in practice, they always will) the situation is entirely different. The sanction for the attempted crime must always be the same, no matter what harm the attempt might have done because the court is unable to determine the probability that an act would lead to harm. One attempt might have been very dangerous, whereas another might be potentially much less

---

[6] The problem here is simple in mathematical terms. There is one equation (for the expected harm/penalty) in two unknowns - the penalties for the attempt and for the crime itself. The solution is indeterminate. The expected penalty will be given by $p_aF_a + p_cF_c$, which, at the optimum, will be equal to the harm inflicted. P_a is the probabilty of an attempted crime resulting from an act, F_a is the penalty for the attempt. P_c and F_c are the probability of occurrence and the penalty for the completed crime itself.

dangerous. But the court is unable to distinguish between these acts.

As a consequence of the court's inability to differentiate between different kinds of attempted crime, the punishment for a minor act might be too severe. Shavell argues that the efficient remedy for this may be to punish the crime itself and not to punish the attempt, provided that the magnitude of the potential harm is not too high. However, if the potential harm is quite large, punishing the crime alone may be insufficient and the attempted crime may also have to be punished. This would occur, for example, if the penalty for the crime itself were set at its maximum level, but the expected penalty is still below the expected harm created by the crime and the attempt to commit it. Unlike the case of perfect information, the penalty for the attempt is now uniquely determined, because the penalty for the crime has already been set. We now have one equation in one unknown (the penalty for the attempted crime). The penalty for the attempt will increase with the probability of the act causing harm and the size of the potential harm, but will in general be less than the penalty for the crime itself.[7]

Finally, it may be important to distinguish between different kinds of attempts. Shavell considers completed attempts and incomplete attempts. An example of a completed attempt would be where someone shoots at another person with the intention of injuring or killing him/her, but the bullet passes harmlessly by and so no harm is caused. Incomplete attempts can be further sub-divided into interrupted attempts and abandoned attempts. An attempt is interrupted if a third person (say, a police officer) intervenes in order to prevent the act from being completed. An abandoned attempt arises when the offender decides not to continue with the original act. Marginal deterrence theory suggests it is only this final category of attempts that might be deterred by having lower penalties for attempted crimes.

Sentences for Repeated Offences

In an ideal world no one would commit crime. In a second-best world, they might do so on one occasion. In the real

---

[7] Interestingly, in a number of recent cases of attempted murder in the UK (Al-Banna, 1984; Hindawi, 1988) no 'discount' was granted because the crime was merely an attempt rather than a completed crime.

world some people commit crimes on many occasions. This raises the question, how should one punish repeat offenders? It is common practice to punish them more severely for the same offence than first-time offenders, but can this be justified? Strangely, there has been little examination of this question in the literature on the economic analysis of punishment. This sub-section draws heavily on the work of Polinsky and Rubinfeld (1989).

In their model, individuals may commit up to two offences and are subject to a fine if caught. The fine for the second offence is allowed to be different from that for the first offence.[8] Polinsky and Rubinfeld show that, in such a situation, social welfare (the social gain of the offender less the harm caused by the offence) is increased by adopting a policy of *increasing* the penalty for repeat offences. The explanation is as follows.

Suppose that individuals differ in their propensity to commit crime. Optimal deterrence – that is, deterring individuals from committing crimes for which the social gain is less than the harm generated – requires that the punishment increase the higher is the individual's offence propensity. However, since the courts are unable to observe individuals' offence propensities, they can punish repeated offences more severely as an indirect means of imposing stiffer penalties on those individuals with higher offence propensities. Individuals with a very low offence propensity will be deterred from committing any crime by a low penalty. On the other hand, those with a higher offence propensity will not be deterred and will commit a first offence. However, they can be deterred from committing a second offence by the imposition of a more severe penalty for second offences.[9]

Is such a policy superior to one which imposes either uniformly high or low penalties for both offences? Polinsky and Rubinfeld show that the 'low-high' strategy is superior to all alternative arrangements of penalties. A high-high or high-low strategy would *over*-deter offences in the first period, whilst

---

[8] Additional assumptions are that (i) individuals are risk neutral, (ii) there is a zero discount rate, and (iii) the probability of detection is one.

[9] Logically there is nothing to stop severity increasing with the number of offences above two, so that the third, fourth and subsequent offences receive even harsher penalties.

a low-low policy would *under*-deter crimes in the second period.[10]

Polinsky and Rubinfeld suggest two other grounds for punishing repeated offences more severely. *First,* more seasoned criminals (repeat offenders) may be able to reduce the probabilty of detection and punishment, so that an increase in the severity of punishment is required in order to maintain the expected level of punishment. *Second,* any stigma attaching to punishment may be subject to diminishing returns and so it may be necessary to impose harsher penalties on repeat offenders in order to offset the declining deterrent effect of the stigma of punishment.

The Criminal Justice Act 1991

In England judges and magistrates have had very considerable discretion in determining the sentences imposed on convicted criminals (Ashworth, 1992). Punishment can serve several aims and it is hardly surprising that experts disagree over the importance of each aim. Economists working in the area of crime and punishment have placed considerable weight on the rôle of punishment as a deterrent to further criminal activity. This is because economists view (potential) criminals as rational self-interested individuals, who respond to incentives in the same way that consumers and producers respond to price signals in the market place (see Section III, pp.21-22). The models and empirical methods favoured by economists have generally not met with the approval of other social scientists, especially criminologists, although some might concede that the activities of 'professional' criminals could be analysed using a model of rational, criminal man.

The underlying principle of the Criminal Justice Act 1991 is one of 'just deserts' – in other words, sentences should be related to the harm caused by the offence[11] – even though, as

---

[10] By over (under) deterrence is meant deterring (not deterring) offences for which the social gain to the offender exceeds (is less than) the harm caused by the offence.

[11] There are some minor exceptions to this rule. Section 1(2)(b) allows the passing of a custodial sentence in order to protect the public and section 2(2)(b) allows the *length* of imprisonment to reflect the need to protect the public, in both cases from death and serious injury.

we have seen, the essential message of the economic approach to punishment is that a sentencing policy based entirely on desert would not necessarily minimise the social cost of crime and its control. Section 2 of the Act states that, where the sentence is a custodial one, it should be

'for such term (not exceeding the permitted maximum) as in the opinion of the court is commensurate with the seriousness of the offence, or of the offence and other offences associated with it'.

Only in the case of violent or sexual offences is incapacitation allowed (Section 2 (2b) of the Act). Under the 1991 Act, deterrence is not a valid argument for exceeding the 'just' sentence. However, the Act contains relatively little elaboration of the term 'seriousness of the offence'.

Legal theorists appear not to be as precise as economists in their formulation of the concept of 'proportionality'. Economists argue that proportionality implies that an offence that is regarded as twice as serious as another should carry twice the sentence (Waldfogel, 1993). According to Ashworth (1992), desert theorists do not see this as necessarily the case. He argues that 'There is no absolute reason why twice the seriousness should lead to twice the sentence...' (p.92), as the scale might be an upward sloping curve with steeply increasing severity for the more serious crimes. Unfortunately, this 'stretched' version of proportionality does not sound like 'just deserts'. Furthermore, if 'stretched' proportionality can be made consistent with desert, then why not 'compressed' proportionality, as in Waldfogel's 'efficient' sentences?[12] Where would this leave the principle of 'just deserts' and the 1991 Act?

Persistent Offenders

Another important feature of the Criminal Justice Act 1991 is the treatment of persistent offenders. Since at least the middle of the last century a predominant theme of sentencing has been the principle of cumulation. Under such a scheme, for

---

[12] In fact, the Act seems to exclude the possibility of 'compressed' proportionality (Ashworth, 1992, p.81).

each new offence committed the sentence is increased above the previous level. As explained above, there is support for such a policy from economic analysis (see previous subsection). However, some 'liberal' legal scholars and judges have expressed concern at the fairness of the cumulative principle (Ashworth, 1992, pp.145-46).[13] As a result, they suggest either flat-rate sentencing (as, for example, with certain parking and traffic offences) or application of the principle of progressive loss of mitigation. However, progressive loss of mitigation also implies that repeated offences are punished more severely than first-time offences. The difference is that the punishment can never exceed the seriousness of the offence, even for the most persistent offender.[14],[15] Accordingly, the maximum permissible sentence for the crime will reflect the harm caused by the offence and first-time offenders receive the maximum mitigation, on the grounds presumably that everyone is allowed at least one mistake. Subsequent offences lead to the progressive loss of mitigation as the commission of further offences indicates that the individual's original criminal act was not out of character.

The principle of progressive loss of mitigation is embodied in Sections 28 and 29 of the Criminal Justice Act 1991. Section 29.1 states that

> 'An offence shall not be regarded as more serious...by reason of any previous convictions of the offender or any failure to respond to previous sentences'.

Section 28 (1) of the Act then allows the court to mitigate the sentence. These two sections, along with other provisions

---

[13] For example, it is claimed that it leads to a double punishment, with the offender being punished for the crime and for previous crimes for which he or she has already been punished. It is also argued that the interests of the public are being put above those of the criminal.

[14] In *Queen* (1981) Mr Justice Jones commented: 'The proper way to look at the matter is to decide on a sentence which is appropriate for the offence for which the prisoner is before the court. Then in deciding whether that sentence should be imposed...the court must have regard to those matters which tell in his favour...and to those matters which tell against him, in particular his record of previous convictions.'

[15] Notable exceptions to the discounting rule for first offences are sentences for more serious crimes, such as murder, armed robbery and rape.

of the Act, are an attempt to apply the principle of progressive loss of mitigation under which the nature of the offence imposes a ceiling on the sentence, which is determined by the seriousness of the offence itself and is not dependent on the offender's prior criminal record. The one exception to this rule allows the court to increase this sentence when previous convictions indicate that the offender is a 'professional' criminal. Unfortunately, the Act neither defines the term 'professional' nor does it elaborate on the extent to which severity might be increased for such offenders.

One particularly controversial aspect of the Criminal Justice Act 1991 was the introduction of so-called 'unit fines'.[16] The Act separated the calculation of the seriousness of the offence (based on a scale from 1 to 50) from the estimation of the financial penalty payable by the offender. The penalty multiplier (£ per unit of seriousness) is then applied to the financial means of the offender, subject to a lower limit of £4 per unit and an upper limit of £100 per unit. Under such a system it is possible for two individuals who have committed the same offence (and on the same number of occasions) to be fined quite different amounts. Is this consistent with the principle of proportionality (or desert)?

Ashworth (1992, p.182) claims there is no inconsistency on the grounds that '... proportionality should only govern the process of estimating the gravity of the offence'. If that is so, then the principle of desert seems capable of being stretched and twisted to such a degree that one wonders if it retains any substance. That said, there is considerable support in the literature on the economic analysis of punishment for setting fines related to the wealth of the offender (see, for example, Becker (1968), Polinsky and Shavell (1984), and the literature on income tax evasion (Pyle, 1991)). Unfortunately, unit fines were one of the reforms in the 1991 Act that were very quickly rescinded.

---

[16] Such a system of monetary punishment is common in Sweden and other Scandinavian countries, where it is known as a 'day fine' system.

V. THE PRIVATISATION DEBATE

At the present time the major organs of the criminal justice system (CJS) – police, courts and prisons – operate primarily within the public sector. Of course, there have always been exceptions, such as private security firms and a small number of private penal establishments.

During the late 1980s there was a noticeable shift of emphasis in UK criminal justice policy – first, away from the public and towards the private provision of crime prevention, and then to the privatisation of the punishment process. This second strand of government policy was particularly noticeable in the White Papers *Punishment, Custody and the Community* (1988) and *Crime, Justice and Protecting the Public* (1990), with their increased emphasis on 'punishment in the community' for non-violent offenders. These ideas were further developed in the Criminal Justice Act 1991. In the last few years there have been several well publicised experiments to privatise certain activities within the CJS, such as employing private security firms to escort offenders from prison to court, operating private prisons, and the hiring by communities of private guards to patrol streets and neighbourhoods. Some of these ideas are discussed below.

In Britain, privatisation has proceeded with the sale of state-owned enterprises, for example, in electricity, gas, and water supply, telecommunications, airlines, airports, coal and railways. It is not a peculiarly British phenomenon, although this country can lay claim to being market leaders. Many other countries have also embarked on privatisation programmes, most notably the former Communist countries of Eastern and Central Europe.

The sale of former state-owned enterprises constitutes the most important form of privatisation. However, privatisation has taken other forms, such as the contracting out of certain services in the public sector, including cleaning and catering services, and even the establishment of 'quasi-markets' in health and social services (see Le Grand and Bartlett, 1993). Given the long period of Conservative Party domination of politics in the UK, it was inevitable that the privatisation (or 'marketisation') spotlight would eventually be turned on other public services. Here we are concerned with services in the CJS, such as policing and penal institutions. However, there are some general arguments about private versus public provision which should first be discussed briefly.

The main arguments against public provision of services concern cost and efficiency. Economists argue that agents in the public sector, insulated from the forces of competition, have little or no incentive to minimise the costs of providing services. Bureaucrats, who possess the 'true' information about costs, are able to hide that information from both their political masters and voters alike. More seriously still, in the absence of competition, it may well be impossible to assess what costs 'should' be. Without adequate incentives, bureaucrats will pursue their own objectives which will frequently conflict with those of the general public (we shall ignore the possibility that politicians and voters might have different objectives from one another). The result is that the level of output will differ from the 'socially optimal' level and the cost of that output will be higher than necessary.

Mueller (1989) surveyed some 50 studies which compare the costs of providing the same services in the public and private sectors (ranging from airlines to weather forecasting) and claims that in over 40 of these studies, public firms '... were found to be significantly less efficient than private firms supplying the same service'. He concludes that '... the evidence that the public provision of a service reduces the efficiency of its provision seems overwhelming'. (p.266). Whilst it is difficult to ensure that like is always being compared with like, where studies have attempted to control for the quality of the good or service offered (for example, house construction) and the scale of operation (for instance, debt collection), the cost differences remain. In the face of such overwhelming empirical evidence it seems clear that there are inefficiencies in public provision.

How might privatisation affect particular parts of the criminal justice system, such as crime prevention, policing, and prisons?

Privatising Crime Prevention

Simply locking doors and closing windows when one leaves home is a crime prevention strategy. Of course, some people adopt more elaborate and expensive precautions such as fitting window locks, installing a safe and having security lighting and/or a burglar alarm fitted. Sometimes there is voluntary group provision of security. For example, residents of three small Gloucestershire villages even grouped together to install a closed circuit television system, in order to monitor suspicious activity, following a spate of burglaries in the villages.[1] In the commercial field, shops and stores employ store detectives, security guards and an increasing number now even install closed circuit television systems to deter shoplifters and fit steel shutters to counteract so-called ram-raiders. Marks & Spencer, for example, reportedly spends over £21 million a year on store security.[2] 'Target hardening', as it has been called, has become extremely popular with certain members of the Government and the Home Office.

Private Provision

In these examples individuals and firms acting on their own initiative are attempting to reduce their chances of becoming the victims of crime. They are in essence buying a 'private' good – crime prevention or protection. But purchase of this good has spillover effects ('externalities') on other individuals. Sometimes these spillovers are good, in that they might persuade potential criminals to give up altogether (and so my purchase of protection benefits others). However, sometimes these spillovers can be harmful. For example, the burglar might be persuaded to give up trying to break into my house but merely moves next door. In other words, my target hardening merely displaces the crime to someone else.

In judging the success of private crime prevention activity from society's point of view, one needs to consider whether such policies merely divert criminals to steal other people's possessions or whether there is a reduction in aggregate crime. Each individual, in deciding whether or not to invest in crime prevention strategies, considers only the costs and benefits to himself or herself, ignoring the costs imposed on and benefits enjoyed by other members of society as a result of such decisions (Carter, 1974). As a result, an individual might

---

[1]   *The Times*, 2 March 1992.

[2]   *The Times*, 23 March 1992.

over-invest (if displacement is a possibility) or under-invest (if deterrence is generated) in crime prevention. To the extent that displacement is not perfect then individuals will *under-invest* in the protection of their own property and so more expenditure on crime prevention would be justified (Carter, 1974; Field and Hope, 1989; and Litton, 1990). Economists are familiar with this problem from studying externalities. The standard argument is that if a good generates beneficial externalities, then its consumption should be subsidised in an attempt to encourage an increase in its use.[3]

One simple device to increase expenditure on crime prevention would be to reduce VAT on home security measures, although this is made more difficult by the moves towards European fiscal harmonisation. Relatively little attention has been paid to the issue of encouraging private expenditure on crime prevention, although Litton (1990) suggested that *theft insurance* might be used to increase incentives for individuals to undertake increased crime prevention expenditures: some insurance companies now offer substantial discounts to customers installing burglar alarms, window locks and security lighting.

Unfortunately, the use of property insurance to encourage private crime prevention raises other, rather difficult, issues. For example, the problem of moral hazard suggests that if I have paid to insure my property against theft, I am *less* likely to take care of it. After all, if it is stolen I can always claim against my insurance policy. Of course, the insurance contract can be redrawn so that if the insurer fails to take proper care (for instance, fails to activate the burglar alarm or leaves windows open) then the insurer is not liable for any losses as a result of crime. Another problem is insurance fraud. I might actually stage a burglary or start a fire in order to claim against my insurance policy or perhaps inflate the value of goods stolen in a genuine break in. To cope with this, insurance companies might offer financial incentives, such as no claims bonuses or excesses on house contents policies, to encourage greater self-protection. An additional benefit of such a policy is that it

---

[3] Recent reports (*Daily Telegraph*, 25 September 1995) on the free supply of locks and other security devices in six crime-prone areas suggest they have reduced crime by between 17 and 60 per cent. The free supply of locks was part of the Government's Safer Cities Programme.

might also encourage the insurance companies to distinguish more clearly between their high-risk and low-risk insurees.

This does not imply that private precautions will fail to reduce crime, but it raises the question whether the better route is through the tax system or the insurance market. The initial conclusion would appear to be that the use of tax incentives is less risky. There is also the question whether *collective* crime prevention (either private or public) might not achieve the same goal more effectively. For example, a group of neighbours could form a Neighbourhood Watch or hire their own private neighbourhood patrol. Would this have a greater deterrent effect than everyone pursuing his or her own private home protection policies? This is an interesting question, which so far has received very little attention from economists (for a purely theoretical analysis in this area, see Shavell, 1991).

Collective Provision

Crime prevention appears to have the characteristics of what economists call a 'public good'. *First*, it is available to everyone in the community in equal (or more or less equal) amounts. It is therefore 'non-rival' in consumption – my consumption of it does not reduce the amount of the good/service available for you to consume. If the police officer patrolling in my street deters someone from breaking into my neighbour's house, he or she probably also dissuades that person from entering illegally into my home. However, police patrolling cannot be a pure public good, because a police officer patrolling my street cannot also be patrolling another street. Clearly, patrolling also has aspects of a private good.

Second, it is 'non-excludable' in the sense that no one can be prevented from enjoying the benefits of the good or service, or at least exclusion is difficult and/or expensive. If I hire someone to patrol near my house, my neighbour may also benefit from this service, because the criminal decides to go to an entirely different neighbourhood. Unfortunately, I cannot prevent my neighbour from enjoying this benefit even if he refuses to join with me in paying for the patrol service. This leads to immediate problems. Even if voluntary collective action (say, hiring a private security firm to patrol the neighbourhood) is more efficient than each individual acting independently (for example, by installing a burglar alarm) there are strong incentives for the optimum solution to break down. This problem is known in game theory as the Prisoners' Dilemma.

Consider the following situation, where for simplicity there are only two households (A and B), who are trying to decide whether to form a Neighbourhood Patrol in their area. The numbers in the cells of Table 6 represent the net gains (benefits less costs) to each household compared with their present situation. The first number in each cell is the gain to household A, whilst the second number is the gain to household B. For example, if both households join the neighbourhood patrol scheme they would each have a net gain of 5. This is the value of any theft/burglary losses prevented minus their costs incurred in hiring the patrol. However, if A joins and B does not, A bears all of the costs and so loses 1. On the other hand, household B reaps some of the benefits at no cost to itself, because potential burglars are deterred from entering B's house by A's purchase of patrolling for the area. Clearly, in these circumstances, B would prefer not to join the scheme and would like A to provide the service for him/her. As each household has the same incentive, neither household is prepared to contribute to the cost of the neighbourhood patrol and, as a result, both are worse off than if the patrol had been formed. That is, they end up in the south-east cell rather than the north-west cell.

In less extreme versions of this problem, known in game theory as the game of chicken, the equilibrium outcome is where one household joins the scheme, but the other stays out. This would happen in the example above if the entries of -1 were replaced by a positive number, for example, 3. The reason for this result is that whilst one's best outcome is being a free-rider on others' public spiritedness, one can still do better by joining than not joining when no one else participates. The 'chicken' game may be a more likely characterisation of participation in voluntary collective crime prevention than is the Prisoners' Dilemma, because it suggests that only some (not all) residents fail to join the scheme.

It has been argued that economists may overstate the extent of the so-called 'free-rider' problem. On the one hand, there is a great deal of experimental evidence to suggest that non-economists are on the whole quite happy to contribute to the provision of public goods (see Frank *et al.*, 1993). On the

TABLE 6:
A Neighbourhood Patrol 'Game'

		Household B	
		Join	Don't Join
Household A	Join	5, 5	−1, 6
	Don't Join	6, −1	0, 0

other hand, game theorists tell us that in infinitely repeated games the co-operative solution (both joining) could emerge if free-riding in any time-period is threatened with a punishment of non-co-operation for the remainder of the game. The potential non-co-operator has then to decide whether a short-term gain is worth the long-term loss of the co-operative gains (see Gibbons, 1992, pp.102-7).

This might be particularly relevant in small communities, where free-riding can be easily detected and punishment can be quite severe (being ostracised by the rest of the community). Certainly, casual empiricism suggests that several attempts to launch private patrols in large, suburban areas have failed to attract widespread support. For example, *The Observer* newspaper (4 July, 1993) reported the example of Sneyd Park in Bristol, where only 1 in 10 of the residents was prepared to pay the £1 per week membership fee. Of course, this may also be part of the learning experience. Once the number of subscribers rises above a critical percentage, and real benefits start to be achieved, then the incentive to join increases. Initially, there may be some scepticism amongst the population about the reliability and quality of the 'product' being offered by a new supplier. Private patrolling is almost unheard of in residential areas in the UK and so there is bound to be some suspicion of the concept at the outset.

Neighbourhood Watch

Neighbourhood Watch (NW) came to the UK from the USA in the early 1980s. Its main objective is the prevention of crime, and particularly burglary. By the end of 1991 there were some 91,000 NW schemes across Great Britain. The schemes are usually funded jointly by the police and the scheme members through voluntary contributions. Whilst each scheme has a designated police contact and contact persons within the scheme who act as liaison with the police, there is a great deal of variation in how the schemes operate (McConville and Shepherd, 1992; Bennett, 1989).

Bennett (1989) undertook a detailed evaluation of two NW schemes in the Acton and Wimbledon areas of London. This entailed 'before and after' interviews in each of the areas to determine, among other things, whether residents had been victims of crime in the previous 12 months. The study included two other areas – a 'displacement' area (on the boundary of the Wimbledon NW scheme) and a 'control' area. Neither the displacement nor the control area had NW schemes in operation. Bennett found that, over the two-year period, recorded crimes rose by 40 per cent in Acton NW (from 57 offences to 80) and fell by 17 per cent in Wimbledon NW (from 81 offences to 67). In the displacement area recorded crimes fell by 9 per cent (from 74 to 67). More importantly, the number of recorded crimes fell in the control area by 39 per cent (from 76 offences to 46).

However, one of the objectives of NW is to encourage the public to act as 'the eyes and the ears of the police', so that if this aim is achieved then the result may be an increase in recorded crime in the NW area and/or a faster rate of increase in recorded crime in the NW compared with other (control) areas. Therefore, 'victim' surveys were carried out in the experimental and control areas to determine the extent of changes in 'true' crime. Unfortunately, the results of the victim surveys show that

'In both experimental areas the incidence of both household and personal victimisations increased from the pre-test to post-test surveys. In the displacement area the rate of both types of offence remained constant, and in the control area the rate went down for household offences and up for offences against the person' (p.98).

Of course, it may be that the period of observation was too short and the number of incidents too small, so that random fluctuations might have caused these results. Another possible explanation is that NW signs on lamp-posts signal rich pickings to potential burglars (rather like burglar alarms are supposed to do), although this is a double-edged sword. The signs also might indicate an increased probability of detection. It is also possible that the increase in crime in the NW areas

[52]

was the result of factors unrelated to the formation of the NW, such as changes in (i) policing policy, and (ii) behaviour of local criminals which were inadequately monitored during the research programme.

The most likely reason for Bennett's finding is that surveillance by the public is extremely difficult, especially in urban communities with transitory populations. Also, there was very little involvement of the average citizen in either of the NW schemes. It is possible that residents in NW schemes become complacent and neglect their property, assuming that their neighbours will look after it for them. Bennett found that few residents attended NW meetings, that more than a half admitted to not looking out for suspicious behaviour, and only a tiny minority either marked their property or requested a home security check. This kind of behaviour clearly constitutes free-riding and would be predicted by economists.

In conclusion, there are two major questions relating to the private provision of crime prevention. *First*, is private (individual) provision more or less efficient than collective provision (whether private or public) in deterring crime? *Second*, if collective provision is more efficient, how can we ensure that all individuals contribute to its cost and an optimum quantity of the good is produced?

Privatising Policing

We have already discussed one aspect of the privatisation of policing when we discussed Neighbourhood Watch and the private provision of police patrols. Here we focus on other aspects of the privatisation of police services. Johnston (1992) refers to the widespread 'civilianisation' of policing that has been taking place recently as one aspect of privatisation. However, the replacement of police officers by civilian staff in areas of police work such as scenes of crime, photography, control room duties hardly constitutes privatisation. Such substitution may reduce the cost to the Exchequer of the police service, but the civilian personnel are still employed in the public sector. Privatisation requires rather more than the mere replacement of uniformed officers by civilian staff. For example, it would need these services to have been contracted out to private companies or to be sold commercially.

Nevertheless, there is scope for some police services to be privatised in this way. Already, services such as cleaning, catering and vehicle maintenance are contracted out to private firms. Recently, the escort and supervision of prisoners was contracted out to Group Four, much to the amusement of the Press when several prisoners escaped. It would be interesting to know how many prisoners escaped whilst being escorted by the police and prison service. We do know that in 1991-92, before privatisation of prison escorting, there were some 473 escapes by prisoners from closed prisons and escorts and that another 1,951 prisoners absconded.[4] Of course, escapes can be reduced by spending more resources on security, but it may not be an efficient use of resources to try to eliminate them.

What else could be done in terms of contracting out? For example, why not privatise the traffic management and control functions, for instance, traffic wardens, by selling these functions to a commercial agency, or granting a licence to collect fines with fine revenues being shared in some way?[5]

In addition to contracting out those police services which are not of a public good nature, one could encourage the police service to sell some of its services on the open market in direct competition with private security firms. For example, why not allow the police to charge for giving advice on the installation of security systems? Likewise, policing of public events could be charged to the organisers at commercial rates. Johnston (1992) argues that the cost of policing football grounds in London was about £8 million in 1987-88, but that the police recouped only some £1 million of this from the football clubs concerned. There seems to be little justification for commercial organisations like these to receive a subsidy from the taxpayer. Other areas suggest themselves, such as the sale of garage services, driving school facilities and the leasing of premises for social functions, provided that there is no interference with essential police functions. Such activities would be undertaken simply to utilise any spare capacity in the facility, consequent on its 'lumpiness'.

Privatisation of Prisons

Several countries have experimented with privatisation of prisons in the last few years, the most notable examples being

---

[4] *Prison Service Annual Report and Accounts*, 1992-93, Cm.2385, London: HMSO, 1993.

[5] Vehicle clamping has already been privatised. - ED.

in the USA, the UK and Australia. Of course, private prisons are not a remotely new idea. In fact, it is only in this century that public provision of prison places has been the norm. Surprisingly, even then elements of a private sector remained in the UK's penal system. For example, private security firms have been running immigration detention centres at major airports since the 1970s.

However, the modern movement to privatise prisons only got underway in the UK in the mid-1980s, following a report from the Adam Smith Institute (cited in McDonald, 1994). Even then, it was not until the late 1980s that the Government announced plans to involve private firms in the operation of remand centres for unsentenced prisoners and/or local prisons for convicted criminals. It was The Criminal Justice Act 1991 that eventually provided the Government with the power to contract out the management of new remand centres and this power was subsequently extended to cover new prisons for convicted criminals and to enable the contracting out of the running of existing prisons. The first contract to be issued was for the operation of The Wolds Remand Centre in Humberside, which opened at the beginning of April 1992.

The term 'private' may be something of a misnomer, for whilst The Wolds is privately owned and managed (by an offshoot of Group Four Security), it operates under contract to the government, being paid £5 million per year in order to house up to 320 remand prisoners. The second private prison to open was Blakenhurst, which is a local prison for sentenced offenders. Here the contract was won by a consortium headed by the Corrections Corporation of America, which operates a number of private prisons in the USA, and the UK construction firms, Mowlem and Sir Robert McAlpine. A further significant development has been the award of a contract to run Strangeways prison in Manchester, an existing prison (albeit much reconstructed following the riots of 1990). In this case the contract was won by the existing management team (the Prison Service).

The debate over private prisons raises a number of issues, which Logan (1990) lists as propriety, cost, quality, flexibility, security, liability, accountability, corruption and dependence. Many of these issues go beyond the scope of this paper and some are not appropriate for economic analysis. Furthermore, at present the number of inmates who are incarcerated in private prisons is only a tiny proportion of the total prison population. For example, in the USA, which has the longest recent experience with prison privatisation, less than 2 per cent of all prisoners are detained in private institutions (McDonald, 1994). When the sample size is so small and the experience of privatisation is so recent it is difficult to see what firm conclusions can be drawn about the success or otherwise of the privatisation programme. The situation is not helped by the lack of information. For example, cost data is not available for the UK's private prisons, because it is regarded as commercially sensitive information (McDonald, 1994). When 'experiments' in the USA, Australia and the UK have progressed somewhat further we will be in a better position to determine whether private prisons represent an improvement over state-run prisons.

In principle, there is nothing wrong with private provision of prison services, provided that they are thoroughly inspected by an independent inspectorate reporting to an independent regulatory authority. After all, there has been a great deal of concern about the degrading, insanitary and antiquated régimes that seem to operate in our present state-run prison system. If we accept that in principle, at least, there is nothing wrong with private prisons, then the question becomes how to design a regulatory system that ensures that we do not get a prison system that is reminiscent of the private prisons which operated in this country from medieval times up to the late 18th century or in the Southern States of the USA in the early part of this century (Borna, 1986). Such a task should not be beyond the wit of mankind. Unfortunately, in this area the discussion tends to be rather more emotive than informative.

In the UK the present interest in private prisons seems to have been fired by a desire to cut costs (McDonald, 1994). However, evidence from the USA is not particularly encouraging about the possibility of cost savings being achieved by a simple switch of ownership from the public to the private domain (Borna, 1986; Weiss, 1989), although McDonald (1994) has questioned the validity of a number of these studies of costs. The situation in the UK may be rather more conducive to the achievement of cost savings through prison privatisation. The present state monopoly of prison operations makes for internal inefficiency, because there is no incentive for managers to reduce costs. The management of the prison system has been unable to tackle the worst excesses of the Prison Officers Association, the trade union for staff employed in the prison system. As a consequence, restrictive practices have thwarted attempts to change the prison system. By breaking the mould, the Government gives power back to the managers of the prisons, so that innovative changes can be undertaken without fear of threats of industrial action. Prison 'firms' will then be free to experiment with alternative régimes and high-tech solutions to security issues, subject to regulatory inspection and control.

On the other hand, *contracting out* prison services will not necessarily save resources. The clue can be found in the literature on rent-seeking (Mueller, 1989). Put simply, the argument is that if a profit can be made from contracting to supply prison services, then potential suppliers of such services have an incentive to 'invest' a sum up to the amount of the potential profit in trying to win the contract. Of course, each potential contractor has exactly the same incentive. It can be shown that in certain circumstances the total amount invested *by all firms* in pursuing the rent (or profit) can exceed the rent available. Hence, the total amount of resources invested by society in prisons might increase as a result of privatisation. Simple comparisons of per-inmate cost in private and public prisons will fail to take these other resource costs into account. This is clearly something that needs to be borne in mind when cost comparisons are eventually possible. Other dangers of contracting out are

- kickbacks to corrupt officials in charge of the tendering process;

- cartels in the tendering process; and

- the formation of interest groups by potential suppliers (Benson, 1990).

Contracting out may not be the best solution to the problem of public sector inefficiency.

The American Experience
The American experience with privatisation and contracting out of criminal justice services has been well surveyed by Benson (1990), who makes a persuasive case for private alternatives to state provision in this area.

Experience with contracting out of police and corrections (prisons) facilities is much longer in the USA, dating back to the mid-1970s. Benson, for example, refers to many local governments which have contracted out the patrolling of parks and other recreational areas, airports and public housing areas. Some *small* communities have even contracted out the whole of their policing functions to private firms. Similarly, many States by the mid-1980s had contracted out to private companies the detention and treatment of low-risk offenders, especially juveniles. Also, in some States public defendant services were contracted out to private law firms.

In all of these areas Benson cites evidence to show considerable cost savings in the provision of services. He argues that these cost savings are achieved because private firms are

- able to adopt a more flexible approach than the government to capital-labour substitution in the production of services;

- forced by competition to seek innovative solutions to problems; and

- can offer the most appropriate size of facility in order to exploit any economies of scale or avoid diseconomies of scale. Moreover, a dissatisfied government purchaser can end the private provider's contract more easily than it can cut public sector jobs.

However, Benson argues that contracting out has possible dangers (see above) and can represent only a second-best solution in many areas of criminal justice activity, such as policing. A more efficient solution is for the citizen to buy these services direct from the private police firm, as has happened in many parts of the USA.

As de Molinari wrote in the 19th century, the

'option the consumer retains of being able to buy security wherever he pleases brings about a constant emulation among all producers, each producer striving to maintain or augment his clientele with the attraction of cheapness or of faster, more complete and better [services]'.[6]

---

[6] Gustave de Molinari, 'De la Production de la Securité', *Journal des Economistes*, 1849, quoted by Benson (1990, p.245).

For example, 85 per cent of citizens of a 25-block area of East Midwood, Brooklyn, contribute to a private neighbourhood patrol. Citizens in parts of St. Louis have even bought their own streets and are responsible for providing their own security patrols.

'In California and Florida, entire developments have been walled and security guards are posted at the gates. Large commercial developments generally have their own security force and traffic enforcement...'[7]

As the figures in Section II show, the USA has been much more successful than other countries in recent years in slowing the rate of increase in crime. Would it be too much to expect that one reason for this has been the switch to private provision of policing and away from public provision?

---

[7] Benson (1990, p.211).

VI. CONCLUSIONS

In recent years there has been an alarming increase in crime – measured by official statistics or by victim surveys – in many advanced, industrialised economies, including Britain. The one notable exception to this trend is the USA, where recorded crime has increased, but 'real' crime appears to be stationary. Many countries now face the dilemma of how to deal with crime at a time when existing criminal justice institutions seem unable to cope with the growing problem.

Although the problem of increasing crime is clear, solutions are less obvious. This *Hobart Paper* has examined research undertaken by *economists* into two main areas of crime – the explanation of criminal activity and the design of punishments for criminal acts. Little is known about this work in the UK, because many of the economists working in this subject are from the USA, where their work has had a significant impact on thinking about crime and criminal justice policy.

The conclusions emerging from this research, especially in the economic analysis of involvement in criminal activity, are clear and unequivocal. Models of criminal behaviour which see criminals as rational individuals are entirely consistent with evidence on crime. Criminals do seem to respond to incentives and punishment does indeed deter. Research on the structure of penalties for convicted offenders shows also that these should be designed carefully to present potential criminals with the 'right' signals. Economists conclude that much greater reliance should be placed on fines and that these should be related to the wealth of the offender. Less emphasis should be placed on imprisonment as a form of punishment, but where imprisonment is used care needs to be exercised in determining sentence lengths so that 'justice' is not bought at the cost of an inefficient allocation of resources.

There seems to be scope for market solutions to the problem of crime. Whether privatisation will make for improvements in the allocation of resources in the fight against crime is as yet too early to say. However, there is no reason in principle why privatisation of some parts of the criminal justice system should not lead to significant cost

[60]

savings and increased efficiency. There is already evidence to show that privatisation has had a substantial effect on incentives in other areas of the economy. There are few areas of crime control and policing where privatisation could not be tried. Unfortunately, there is a great deal of prejudice and vested interest to be overcome before some of the main players in the criminal justice system will be prepared to accept privatisation. Experiments in the prison field will eventually help to overcome these entrenched positions.

As the research cited in Section III shows, criminals are deterred by the prospect of capture, but public policing has failed to deter property-related offences. This should not be surprising and is not meant to be a criticism of the police. Catching burglars and thieves in the act is only a remote possibility. Once the act has been committed, catching the perpetrators is almost a matter of luck or chance. Faced by this prospect, public policy can offer only increased severity of punishment, but that option is fraught with difficulties (not least, the cost). A more realistic approach is to accept that crime prevention is best achieved by individuals acting in their own interests. In this the state can aid and facilitate their actions by, for example, providing tax incentives to encourage individuals to improve the security of their own property and to purchase private policing services.

It has been suggested that incentives should be offered to the public police and prison services to encourage them to solve crime and to reform convicted offenders respectively. The danger with this suggestion is that it will merely serve to encourage these bodies to massage the figures. For example, crimes can be 'solved' by getting innocent people to confess to them. Likewise recidivists can be kept out of the criminal justice system by corrupt officials whose financial interests are served by doing so.

The real problem is that 'producers' in the criminal justice system are not directly answerable to their customers (the victims of crime). As a result, they can pursue their own interests which may conflict with those of the victims. The solution will be when the consumer can choose to buy protection in the market-place. An unhappy consumer will then have the power of exit, either by moving to another area or by firing the present supplier and hiring another one.

QUESTIONS FOR DISCUSSION

1. Why might individuals fail to report crimes committed against them to the police? How might incentives to report crimes be improved?
2. Discuss the value of statistics on recorded crime and clear-up rates as measures of police effectiveness. What alternative measures would you suggest?
3. What evidence is there in favour of the hypothesis that criminals respond to incentives?
4. Why might changes in (recorded) crime be *inversely* related to changes in indicators of economic activity in the short term, but *positively* related to those same indicators over the long term?
5. Should the punishment for a crime be proportionate to the harm caused by the offence? Why might this 'rule' fail to produce an 'efficient' outcome?
6. Which services provided by the Criminal Justice System are of a 'public good' nature and which are of a 'private good' kind?
7. Why would you expect the private provision of policing functions to be cheaper than public provision of the same services?
8. What are the main obstacles to private provision in the Criminal Justice system?

REFERENCES/FURTHER READING

Allan, E.A., and D.J. Steffensmeier (1989): 'Youth, underemployment and property crime: Differential effects of job availability and job quality on juvenile and young adult arrest rates', *American Sociological Review*, Vol.54, pp.107-23.

Ashworth, A. (1992): *Sentencing and Criminal Justice*, London: Weidenfeld and Nicolson.

Becker, G.S. (1968): 'Crime and punishment: an economic approach', *Journal of Political Economy*, Vol.76, pp.169-217.

Bennett, T. (1989): *Evaluating Neighbourhood Watch*, Aldershot, Hants.: Gower.

Benson, B.L. (1990): *The Enterprise of Law: Justice Without the State*, San Francisco: Pacific Research Institute for Public Policy.

Block, M.K., and J.M. Heineke (1975): 'A labor theoretic analysis of criminal choice', *American Economic Review*, Vol.65, pp.314-25.

Borna, S. (1986): 'Free enterprise goes to prison', *British Journal of Criminology*, Vol.26, pp.321-43.

Box, S. (1987): *Recession, Crime and Punishment*, London: Macmillan.

Burrows, J. (1982): 'How crimes come to police notice', *Home Office Research and Planning Unit Research Bulletin*, No.13, pp.12-15.

Cameron, S. (1988): 'The economics of crime and deterrence: a survey of theory and evidence', *Kyklos*, Vol.41, pp.301-23.

Cantor, D., and K.C. Land (1985): 'Unemployment and crime rates in post-World War II United States: a theoretical and empirical analysis', *American Sociological Review*, Vol.50, pp.317-32.

Carr-Hill, R.A., and N.H. Stern (1979): *Crime, The Police and Criminal Statistics*, London: Academic Press.

Carter, R.L. (1974): *Theft in the Market*, Hobart Paper No.60, London: Institute of Economic Affairs.

Chiricos, T.G. (1987): 'Rates of crime and unemployment: an analysis of aggregate research evidence', *Social Problems*, Vol.34, pp.187-212.

Cohen, M. (1988): 'Pain, suffering and jury awards: a study of the cost of crime to victims', *Law and Society Review*, Vol.22, pp.537-55.

Cooter, R., and T. Ulen (1988): *Law and Economics*, London: HarperCollins.

Cover, J.P., and P.D. Thistle (1988): 'Time series, homicide and the deterrent effect of capital punishment: the US and Canadian experience', University of Alabama Discussion Paper.

Deadman, D.F., and D.J. Pyle (1989): 'Homicide in England and Wales: a time series analysis, University of Leicester Discussion Paper.

Deadman, D.F., and D.J. Pyle (1993): 'The effect of the abolition of capital punishment in Great Britain: an application of intervention analysis', *Journal of Applied Statistics*, Vol.20, pp.191-206.

Deadman, D.F., and D.J. Pyle (1995): 'Forecasting recorded property crime using a time-series econometric model', University of Leicester Public Sector Economics Discussion Paper, pp.12, forthcoming, October 1995.

van Dijk, J.J.M., and P. Mayhew (1992): *Criminal Victimisation in the Industrialised World*, Ministry of Justice, The Netherlands.

Ehrlich, I. (1973): 'Participation in illegimate activities: a theoretical and empirical analysis', *Journal of Political Economy*, Vol.81, pp.521-64.

Ehrlich, I. (1975): 'The deterrent effect of capital punishment: a question of life and death', *American Economic Review*, Vol.65, pp.397-417.

Ehrlich, I. (1977): 'Capital punishment and deterrence: some further thoughts and evidence', *Journal of Political Economy*, Vol.85, pp.741-88.

Farrington, D., B. Gallagher, L. Morley, R. Ledger, and D. West, (1986): 'Unemployment, School-Leaving and Crime', *British Journal of Criminology*, Vol.26, pp.335-56.

Field, S. (1990): *Trends in Crime and Their Interpretation. A Study of Recorded Crime in Post-War England and Wales*, Home Office Research Study No.119.

Field, S., and T. Hope (1989): 'Economics and the market in crime prevention', *Home Office Research Bulletin*, No.26, pp.40-44.

Frank, R.H., T. Gilovich, and D.T. Regan (1993): 'Does studying economics inhibit co-operation?', *Journal of Economic Perspectives*, Vol.7, pp.159-72.

Freeman, R.B. (1980): 'Crime and Unemployment', in J.Q. Wilson (ed.), *Crime and Public Policy*, pp.89-106.

Friedman, D., and W. Sjostrom (1993): 'Hanged for a sheep – the economics of marginal deterrence', *Journal of Legal Studies*, Vol.22, pp.345-66.

Gibbons, R. (1992): *A Primer in Game Theory*, Brighton, Sussex: Harvester Wheatsheaf.

Le Grand, J., and W. Bartlett (1993): *Quasi-Markets and Social Policy*, London: Macmillan.

Granger, C.W.J., and P. Newbold (1986): *Forecasting Economic Time-Series*, London: Academic Press Inc., 2nd edn.

Hakim, C. (1982): 'The social consequences of high unemployment', *Journal of Social Policy*, Vol.11, pp.433-67.

Hale, C., and D. Sabbagh (1991): 'Testing the relationship between unemployment and crime: a methodological comment and empirical analysis using time-series data for England and Wales', *Journal of Research in Crime and Delinquency*, Vol.28, pp.400-17.

Henry, A.F., and J.F. Short (1954): *Homicide and Suicide*, Glencoe, Illinois: Free Press.

[65]

Home Office (1988): *Punishment, Custody and The Community*, Cmnd.424, London: HMSO.

Home Office (1990): *Crime, Justice and Protecting The Public*, Cmnd.965, London: HMSO.

Hough, M., and P. Mayhew (1983): *The British Crime Survey: first report*, Home Office Research Study, No.76.

Johnston, L. (1992): *The Rebirth of Private Policing*, London: Routledge.

Klein, L.R., B.E. Forst, and V. Filatov (1978): 'The deterrent effect of capital punishment: an assessment of the estimates', in A. Blumstein, J. Cohen, and D. Nagin (eds.), *Deterrence and Incapacitation: Estimating the Effects for Criminal Sanctions on Crime Rates*, National Academy of Sciences.

Leamer, E.F. (1983): 'Let's take the con out of econometrics', *American Economic Review*, Vol.73, pp.31-43.

Lewis, D.E. (1986): 'The general deterrent effect of longer sentences', *British Journal of Criminology*, Vol.26, pp.47-62.

Litton, R.A. (1990): *Crime and Crime Prevention for Insurance Practice*. Aldershot, Hants.: Avebury.

Logan, C.H. (1990): *Private Prisons*, Oxford University Press.

Long, S.K., and A.D. Witte (1983): 'Current economic trends: implications for crime and criminal justice', in K.N. Wright (ed.), *Crime and Criminal Justice in a Declining Economy*, pp.69-143.

Maxfield, M. (1987): *Explaining Fear of Crime*, Home Office Research and Planning Unit Paper No.43.

Mayhew, P., N.A. Maung, and C. Mirrlees-Black (1993): *The 1992 British Crime Survey*, Home Office Research Study No.132.

McConville, M., and D. Shepherd (1992): *Watching Police Watching Communities*, London: Routledge.

McDonald, D.C. (1994): 'Public imprisonment by private means', *British Journal of Criminology*, Vol.34, pp.29-48.

McManus, W.S. (1985): 'Estimates of the deterrent effect of capital punishment: the importance of the researcher's prior beliefs', *Journal of Political Economy*, Vol.93, pp.417-25.

Mueller, D.C. (1989): *Public Choice II*, Cambridge University Press.

Passell, P., and J.B. Taylor (1977): 'The deterrent effect of capital punishment: another view', *American Economic Review*, Vol.67, pp.445-51.

Polinsky, A.M., and D.L. Rubinfeld (1989): 'A model of optimal fines for repeat offenders', Stanford Working Paper No.51.

Polinsky, A.M., and S. Shavell (1984): 'The optimal use of fines and imprisonment', *Journal of Public Economics*, Vol.24, pp.89-99.

Pyle, D.J. (1983): *The Economics of Crime and Law Enforcement*, London: Macmillan.

Pyle, D.J. (1989): 'The economics of crime in Britain', *Economic Affairs*, Vol.9, pp.6-9.

Pyle, D.J. (1991): 'The economics of taxpayer compliance', *Journal of Economic Surveys*, Vol.5, pp.165-98.

Pyle, D.J., and D.F. Deadman (1993): 'Assessing the impact of legal reform using intervention analysis', *International Review of Law and Economics*, Vol.13, pp.193-215.

Pyle, D.J., and D.F. Deadman (1994a): 'Crime and unemployment in Scotland: some further results', *Scottish Journal of Political Economy*, Vol.41, pp.314-24.

Pyle, D.J., and D.F. Deadman (1994b): 'Property crime and the business cycle in post-war Britain', *British Journal of Criminology*, Vol.34, pp.339-57.

Reilly, B., and R. Witt (1992): 'Crime and unemployment in Scotland', *Scottish Journal of Political Economy*, Vol.39, pp.213-28.

Sah, R. (1991): 'Social osmosis and patterns of crime', *Journal of Political Economy*, Vol.99, pp.1,272-95.

Shavell, S. (1985): 'Criminal law and the optimal use of nonmonetary sanctions as a deterrent', *Columbia Law Review*, Vol.85, pp.1,232-62.

Shavell, S. (1990): 'Deterrence and the punishment of attempts', *Journal of Legal Studies*, Vol.19, pp.435-66.

Shavell, S. (1991): 'Individual precautions to prevent theft: private versus socially optimal behaviour', *International Review of Law and Economics*, Vol.11, pp.123-32.

Shavell, S. (1992): 'A note on marginal deterrence', *International Review of Law and Economics*, Vol.12, pp.345-55.

Stigler, G. (1970): 'The optimum enforcement of laws', *Journal of Political Economy*, Vol.78, pp.526-36.

Tarling, R. (1982): 'Crime and Unemployment', *Home Office Research and Planning Bulletin*, No.12.

Thomas, D.S. (1927): *Social Aspects of The Business Cycle*, New York: Gordon and Breach.

Waldfogel, J. (1993): 'Criminal sentences as endogenous taxes: are they "just" or "efficient"?', *Journal of Law and Economics*, Vol.36, pp.139-51.

Weiss, J. (1989): 'Private prisons and the state', in R. Matthews (ed.), *Privatising Criminal Justice*, London: Sage.

Willis, K.G. (1983): 'Spatial variations in crime in England and Wales: testing an economic model', *Regional Studies*, Vol.17, pp.261-72.

Wolpin, K.I. (1978a): 'An economic analysis of crime and punishment in England and Wales, 1894-1967', *Journal of Political Economy*, Vol.86, pp.815-40.

Wolpin, K.I. (1978b): 'Capital punishment and homicide in England: a summary of results', *American Economic Review*, Vol.68, pp.422-27.